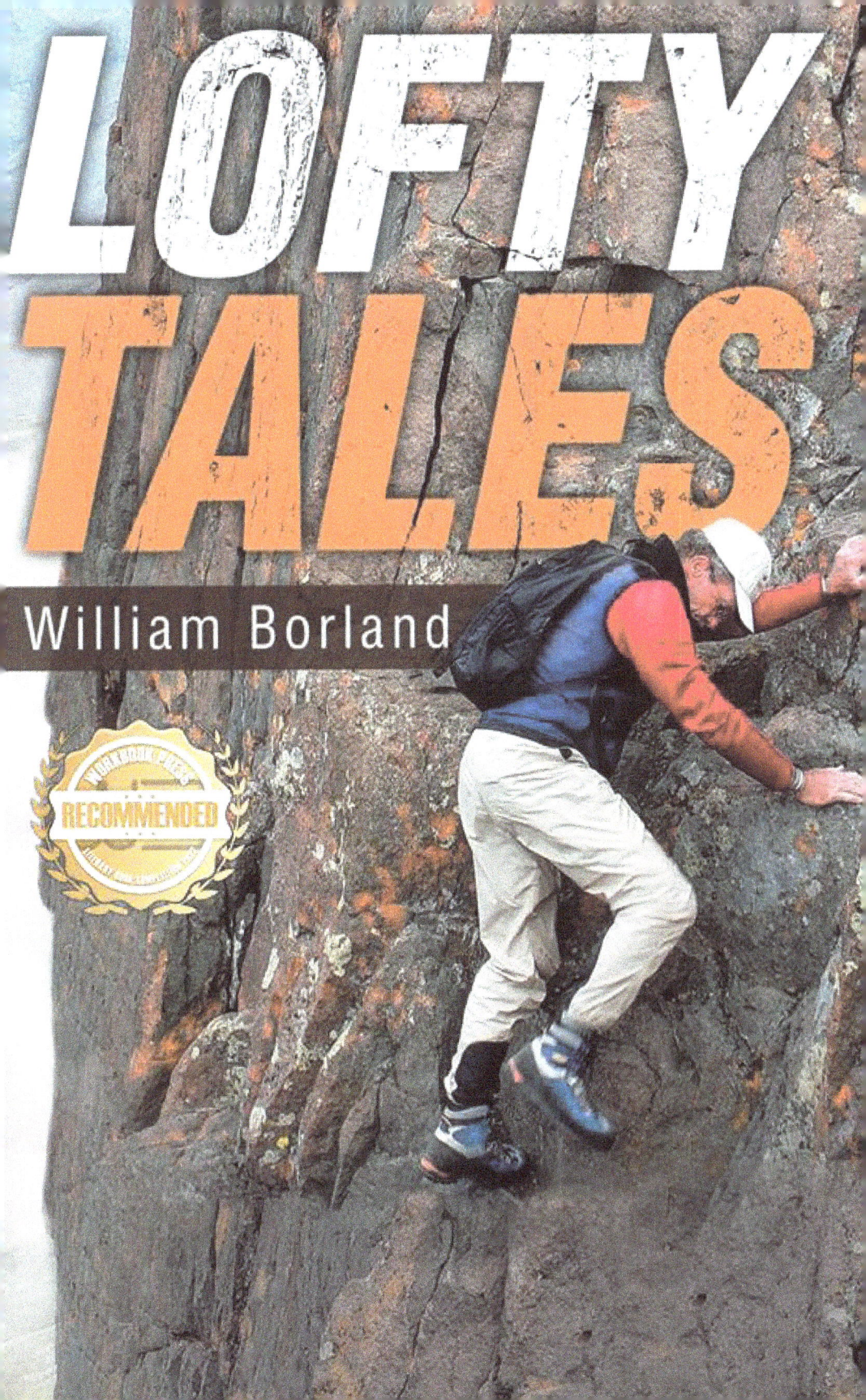

LOFTY TALES

William Borland

WORKBOOK PRESS LLC
187 E Warm Springs Rd,
Suite B285 Las Vegas NV 89119 USA

Website: https://workbookpress.com/
Hotline: 1-888-818-4856
Email: admin@workbookpress.com

Ordering Information:
Quantity sales. Special discounts are available on quantity purchases by corporations, associations, and others.
For details, contact the publisher at the address above.

ISBN-13:   978-1-961845-47-3 Paperback Version
             978-1-961845-46-6 Digital Version

REV. DATE: 11/15/2023

LOFTY TALES

by

William C. Borland

Tucson, Arizona

"Remembrance of things past is not necessarily the remembrance of things as they were." Marcel Proust

Seeking adventure? You don't have to look for it; just spend time outdoors and it will find you.

Dedication

This book is dedicated to five people who will always be very close to my heart:

Allison May, Laura May, Corinne May

and

Jack Borland, Reese Borland

Preface

This writing is at the request of my children and grandchildren and they are its principal audience. They have asked that I make an attempt to document some of the details of my many mid-life outdoor adventures around the country and around the world before they get totally lost in the fog of old age.

The reconstruction of the story details here is aided by many notebooks that documented the trip details daily as they occurred. That doesn't mean that they are without error, but rather that any errors here are inadvertent.

After long thought I have elected to also include a summary description of two years of my life in uniform simply because that experience had a greater influence on the personality that I grew into than any other single event in my life.

Mark Twain is credited with having developed the notion that one shouldn't ever let the truth stand in the way of a good story! So, as always, it is left to the reader to decide how best to enjoy these adventures. But, more importantly, I hope that they serve as an incentive to the reader to learn to live life to its fullest every single day. It's a wonderful, exciting, challenging, and rewarding world out there. Don't waste a single day discovering that.

And, finally, I offer many thanks to my good friend, Neil Barrett, for the cover photo from our climb together in Colorado. It is used here with his permission. And a special thanks to Sandra Rousseau for her timely proofreading skills.

Table of Contents

Chapter One

Introduction

I guess that outdoor adventuring has been in my blood since my earliest years. My introduction to Boy Scouts was marked by the discovery of scout ranks and merit badges that rewarded successfully completing various outdoor tasks such as hiking, camping, fire building, compass and map orienteering, nature species identification and the like. Growing up in the country certainly encouraged development of outdoor skills as well.

But this all took a more committed turn when I left graduate school, completed my commitment to the US Army, and started my first real job working for IBM in New York State.

Now I had the time and money, as well as the continued interest, to get into backpacking and hiking more regularly. Running around with a group of friends who were also into backpacking, canoeing, kayaking, and cross country skiing certainly helped, too.

We had access to the Adirondack State Park in upstate New York, the country's largest state park, which offered endless hiking trails, camping opportunities, and water ways suitable for canoeing, rafting, and kayaking.

The Adirondack Mountain Club (ADK), in order to encourage hiking and backpacking throughout the entire park, rather than only in selected trails around Mt. Marcy, the state's highpoint, offered a "merit badge" to anyone who managed to summit each of the park's 46 highest peaks. Achieving this made one an official "ADK 46'R" with a sew-on badge to prove it.

Since I quickly became the "go to" guy in our group for planning the next weekend's outdoor activity, I was easily the first in our group to achieve the ADK 46'R award – completed in only two years of weekend hikes. Others quickly followed my lead by influencing my selection of subsequent hikes to their advantage.

I started a practice within our group that added a lot of fun to our Adirondack hiking ventures. As I approached my 46th and final Adirondack peak, I encouraged my friends to join me on that hike by announcing that we would have a big celebration on top. And when that time came, on top of wind and snow-blown Whiteface Mountain, I laid out a linen tablecloth, linen napkins, long-stemmed glassware, and a bottle of champagne. (I had gotten the idea from an old Adirondack Mountain Club newsletter where they always staged a special celebration when a member achieved his 46 climbs.) We needed rocks to hold down the napkins and tablecloth because the wind was howling, but we celebrated in style – and froze in the cold wind. But we had started a fun tradition.

A brief year later my good friend Lennie Carpenter had hiked 45 of the listed peaks and had invited all of us to join him on his hike to the top of Algonquin Peak, his 46th. I then announced that we would agree to join him on his final mountain hike provided that he "one upped" my earlier celebration. He reluctantly agreed and so on top he broke out a linen tablecloth, linen napkins, long-stemmed glassware, and champagne, to which he added cheese and crackers. We voted and agreed that he had appropriately "one upped" my celebration from a year ago.

A short six months later another good hiking friend, Richard Kast, announced that he was making plans to hike up his 46th peak and wanted all of us to join him. I reminded him of his obligation to continue our informal tradition. He agreed and soon we all were off to the summit.

At one point, when we stopped for a break on the way up, Richard continued on to the summit – greeting us as we arrived a few minutes later. He, too, had once more brought along the expected linen tablecloth and napkins, appropriate glassware, champagne, cheese and crackers – and a candelabra – and asked if that would suffice. I thought about it for a brief moment and announced that he would indeed have satisfied the "one-up-man-ship" requirement – provided that the candelabra candles were lit. This would be no small requirement since the wind had been blowing strong all morning. But, at precisely that moment, the wind stopped, the candles were successfully lit, appropriate photos were taken, and the "one-up-man-ship" requirement had been satisfied.

But, as it turned out, our fun wasn't over. Upon returning to our cars at the bottom of the mountain, we were surprised by a second celebration - this one prepared by Richard's girlfriend - with a fancy lace tablecloth laid over the hood of one of the cars upon which was placed a spread of caviar and crackers together with glasses and a bottle of Dom Perignon. We were celebrating in style! But we were also planting seeds of worry in the minds of those in our group who had yet to complete their 46 peaks – afraid that by the time that they were to earn their own such celebration, they would need to haul up tables, chairs, and a dancing band! It was great fun!

Soon, the more adventurous of us branched out to hike the highpoints of Vermont, New Hampshire, and Maine, and then discussed how we might tackle a hike along the length of the 2160 mile long Georgia-to-Maine Appalachian Trail.

While the summers and fall in New York were ideal for hiking and backpacking, the spring was ideal for white water canoeing once the snow melt raised the many local placid streams to roaring capacity. This led to a natural extension into kayaking – using fiberglass kayaks that we built ourselves using a hand-fabricated set of molds. These boats were equal or even stronger than commercially-built rigs – and they needed to be because we gave them quite a workout.

We also discovered that in the usually placid Lehigh River in northeastern Pennsylvania, the Corps of Engineers scheduled a special large release of water from their Lehigh Dam one weekend each month providing a predictably roaring playground for white water canoeing and kayaking down river each month. That experience in particular taught me many more ways to get out of a canoe in a hurry!

But this enthusiasm for boating also led me into planning week long canoe trips for our group to New England or Canada every summer. In 1970, one year after starting work in Poughkeepsie, New York, several of us canoed for a week down the Allagash River in northern Maine in the newly opened Allagash Wilderness. In both 1971 and 1972 I pulled together week long canoeing trips into the Algonquin Provincial Park in Ontario, Canada, and in 1973 and 1974 we enjoyed canoeing adventures in La Verendrye Reserve and the Kipawa Wilderness in Quebec Province. In 1975 we spent a week canoeing down the West Branch of the Penobscot River in Maine - this time with the whole family in the canoe when the kids were six and eight – followed a year later with a family canoe trip back to the Algonquin Park. This gave them their first exposure in the wild to wolves, moose, beavers, otters, and the famous northern lights. We even had a chance to experience "foxfire" in the wild. (Foxfire is phosphorescent light emitted by special bioluminescent fungi growing on decaying timber).

On our trips into Canada it was not uncommon to get far enough north that the people there only spoke French instead of English. And on our trip into the Kipawa Wilderness, the people there didn't even speak French, but rather spoke their native Cree language. That was exotic for us for sure.

In 1978 I successfully negotiated a job transfer to Tucson, Arizona, to join a brand new IBM product development laboratory being built there. This opened up a whole new set of outdoor opportunities such as rafting, hunting, and horseback riding, but uphill hiking remained paramount. In short order I had been in and out of the Grand Canyon, hiked to Humphreys Peak, Arizona's highpoint at 12,633 feet, and any number of Colorado's 14,000 foot peaks.

In due time I managed to summit the highpoints of California, New Mexico, Texas, Nevada, Colorado, Oregon, Washington, Idaho, Utah, Wyoming, and Montana along with, eventually, 44 of Colorado's fifty eight 14,000 foot peaks. I was on a roll, and having great fun, but as of 1986 I had not yet hiked outside of the contiguous United States.

This was about to change with the publication of the book Seven Summits in 1986. This book was the story of how two middle-aged, white-collar executives, Frank Wells and Dick Bass, decided to try to be the first to summit all seven of the continental highpoints. While each of these seven peaks had already been successfully climbed, no one person had climbed all seven of them. They wanted to be the first. Their story here made these summits look to be achievable by mere mortals, even including Mt. Everest, without having super-human climbing strength or skills.

Ultimately, the popularity of this book, detailing their successful odyssey, permanently revolutionized the international mountain guiding business. Now virtually every mountain guiding service around the world offers guided climbs to all of these seven summits every year.

I received a copy of <u>Seven Summits</u> from my daughter and son, Robin and Scott, for my reading pleasure and, to their surprise, within a year I was on my way to Alaska to make an attempt on Mt. McKinley (now officially renamed Denali), the highpoint of North America, at 20,306 feet.

At that point I had no particular interest in climbing the other six peaks, but Mt. McKinley had particular appeal simply because it was North America's highest. Thus began an adventure odyssey that was to eventually take me all over the world. That was 1987 and I was 45 years old.

Chapter Two

Continental Highpoints

Mt. McKinley (North America)

I had signed on with Genet Expeditions, a mountain guiding service, headquartered in Wasilla, Alaska, with considerable experience guiding clients up Mt. McKinley. The chief guide for our group of four clients was Vern Tejas, a Texan transplant, well on his way to forging a reputation for stamina, unique personality, and good climbing judgement. He had already climbed Mt. McKinley eleven or twelve times, had participated in several key mountain rescues there, and was often consulted on other rescue efforts. Our assistant guide, John Schweider, who I was to meet up with again a few years later, had already successfully guided on Mt. McKinley three times previously. I was on a good team.

I was clearly under-qualified to climb on a mountain that was 20,310 ft. tall in seriously steep snow and ice conditions in sub-freezing temperatures with a "climbing resume" that only included 14,000 ft. climbs in Colorado and California in the summer, but Genet Expeditions accepted my application anyway and I was on my way. (Genet Expeditions eventually lost their license from the U.S. Park Service to guide on Mt. McKinley because of their lax acceptance requirements and are no longer in business.)

I travelled to Alaska at the end of April in 1987. After the required equipment and clothing reviews, and an interview by Lew Freedman, (Freedman was a reporter from the Anchorage Times who was writing what was going to be a full page spread on mountain climbing on Mt. McKinley), we flew onto the Kahiltna Glacier at 7100 ft. elevation with a ski plane, just below McKinley's peak and twenty-some trail miles from its summit. (Flying onto this glacier obviated a three-to-four week slog by foot through tundra, bogs, and dangerous glaciers in order to start the actual climb of the mountain. In fact, this flight destination is so popular, that it is often referred to as the Kahiltna International Airport for all of the international teams flying in there over the short climbing season.) The summit was easily visible from our base camp. The temperature was well below freezing. We had used Talkeetna Air Taxi Service, piloted by owner and chief pilot, Lowell Thomas, Jr, former lieutenant governor of Alaska and son of the famous international correspondent Lowell Thomas, Sr. As a child Lowell Jr. had often vacationed with his family in Tucson and so we had plenty to talk about.

Lew Freedman joined us on the mountain for an hour or so in order to get some shots for his upcoming newspaper article of our base camp, the mountain peak itself, and our fearless leader, Vern. I told Vern that I, too, wanted to be famous like him and so when Lew was setting up for a final shot of Vern with McKinley in the background, I joined him in the shot, already dreaming of finding my picture on the front page of the Anchorage Daily News one day soon.

Our group consisted of our guide and assistant guide, Vern and John, two fellows from Anchorage, Tony and Larry, and me. We were still expecting the arrival of a fourth climber, Mary, from Seattle, who was by now a couple days late. And so our expedition (and radio call sign) became known as the "Missing Mary Expedition" and we were stuck with that moniker for the rest of our trip. She eventually did show - on a special flight from Talkeetna - just before we were to leave base camp and head up the mountain. She was bundled up from head to toe and for the remainder of our trip we wondered what she actually looked like beneath all of that nylon, down and sunblock.

We set up Camp 1, our base camp, with mountaineering tents surrounded by 4 – 5 foot high walls of ice blocks, that we had to cut with a special ice saw, to provide needed protection from the high winds. Our climbing plan called for us to carry a load of supplies, mostly food and gas, by snowshoe, up the glacier a day's hike away, stash it, and return to our tent site. The following day we'd break camp and haul it up to our supply cache establishing there a new camp – complete with more ice block walls. This way we moved slowly up the mountain with a new campsite every two days while, at the same time, getting acclimatized to the slowly increasing elevation. To help us with our heavy loads, we carried half our assigned weight in our backpacks and half in orange plastic sleds that we pulled behind us. These sleds were also useful in speeding up our return to our lower camp. Picture six climbers, all roped to one another, on sleds, careening down an icy snow slope, with snowshoes, ski poles, and ice axes flying every which way. It was hilarious!

On one of the days out on the glacier we had light snowfall together with high winds creating a complete whiteout which completely obscured our route. Even the wands that we had placed to mark our route were not visible. We were forced to travel by compass hoping that we'd manage to find our way back to our tent site. It was touch and go for a time.

We were never away from our tents without being roped to one another lest we tumble into an unmarked crevasse – of which there were plenty. Our Camp 2 was at an elevation of about 7700 ft., Camp 3 at around 9600 ft., and Camp 4 at about 12,000 ft. From there the route started to get very steep finally arriving at Camp 5, a large open ice field, at 14,200 ft. at the foot of the famous West Buttress. A dozen other international climbing teams were already established there. It was like the United Nations on Ice with groups from Great Britain, Wales, Austria, Australia, Romania, and Switzerland among others! There was even a large medical tent manned by doctors, including Dr. Peter Hackett, author of the popular book, "Mountaineering Medicine," who were studying the variety of altitude illnesses that climbers are plagued with.

Now temperatures dropped regularly below zero – with temperatures at the summit reported to be around -30° F. Our weather was holding, with only occasional light snow, and we were right on schedule having established and moved five camps in ten days. We were able to walk with snowshoes as far as Camp 4, but the 30 – 40 degree slope to Camp 5 required that we finally break out our crampons and ice axes. I was clearly out of my element here – never having experienced anything like this before, but, so far, I hadn't run into anything that I couldn't handle. At this point many of the various expeditions had attempted to summit, but so far, none had made it on our West Buttress route. And, as far as we knew, only one expedition had made it up a different route, because of the high winds and cold weather up high.

That next day we carried a load of five days' worth of food and gas up the very steep wall of the West Buttress to its top where we stashed our load and started to prepare a campsite, Camp 6, at 16,300 ft. before returning to Camp 5. For the first time, because of the extreme steepness, we attached ourselves to rope that had been fixed to the mountain wall lest we slip and take our whole team down the mountain with us. We used it both going up the wall as well as for descending.

At what had become our routine, with the weather still holding, we broke camp the following day and moved up to Camp 6. We were getting pretty good at this routine. And, you guessed it, the following day yet again we broke camp and moved up to our final high camp, Camp 7, to the so called "Football Field" at 17,200 ft. This required negotiating a very narrow ridgeline with very steep drop-offs of thousands of feet on either side of us. This final camp was referred to as the Football Field because we were tented on a large platform easily as big as a football field with several thousand feet of vertical drop offs on the sides.

Now we were finally staged for a summit attempt the following day, health and weather holding, after having been on the mountain for just under two weeks. And we had several days' worth of food and gas to play with. That's when our good weather luck ran out. We had just experienced almost two weeks of stable, even if cold, weather, and that is unheard of in northern Alaska. The wind was building in the morning with temperatures around minus 20° F.

That first night the winds came up and blew down our make-shift ice block wall protecting our tents, necessitating a rapid, midnight effort to rebuild these walls, double thick this time, in -20° F temps, before getting back to our sleeping bags. That was a lot of ice block sawing in the dark! One other group near us had their tent destroyed by the wind and so they moved to a snow cave that they quickly dug for themselves.

This storm stayed with us for five days before letting up enough to give us a shot at the summit. Those were five long days since we had virtually nothing to do but lie in our sleeping bags and try to sleep. We quickly read through all of the books that each climber had brought along. Each night we made preparations to go for the summit early the next morning, by melting snow for water, planning our food needs, and laying out our climbing gear – only to be disappointed five mornings in a row as the storm continued. We ran out of food and fuel after several days and had to search for and dig up stashes left by expeditions from earlier years.

On Day 6 at this high camp, our 17th day on the mountain, there was a break in the weather and finally we made a bid for the summit. We did make it up to Denali Pass at 18,200 ft. before losing our first climber, Tony, to some sort of odd altitude issue affecting his cognitive function. (He couldn't even tell us his name or count the fingers on his hand!) He got escorted back to camp by John, our assistant guide, while Vern continued to lead the remaining three of us on to the summit. But it was not to be.

About 1,000 ft. shy of the summit Vern got a radio call reporting that another storm was on its way toward us and was expected to be severe. (Are there ever storms on Mt. McKinley that are not severe?) We counseled. Vern called for a vote on whether to continue or turn back. Larry called for a retreat while Mary wanted to continue. Vern announced that mine would be the tie-breaker vote. I really wanted to make the summit after all of that waiting, but this being my very first time at this elevation, I deferred to his experience and judgement. He didn't hesitate a bit, immediately turned around, and led us back to camp where we made immediate plans to begin our retreat to Camp 5 at 14,200 ft. at first light. We quickly discovered that the other groups camping on the Football Field with us were already making plans to bail as quickly as practical.

Once back at Camp 5, as the storm hit, we recovered some of our stashed food and fuel and continued in a total whiteout down to Camp 4 around 13,000 ft. where we quickly set up one tent with a single ice block wall to block the wind and tucked into the tent. With difficulty we prepared some hot soup – our first food since leaving the Football Field.

Other climbing groups were bailing out left and right as well.

Along the way down to Camp 4, Larry, who was in the lead, stepped into a crevasse, in the middle of a complete white out, and disappeared up to his ears. I had him secured on my rope and so we were quickly able to help him get out, but it certainly put the fear of God in him.

Before we got our second tent set up at Camp 4 there was a brief lull in the storm and so I suggested to Vern that we take advantage of that lull and continue down the glacier toward Camp 1. We had already had all of the fun on that mountain that we could stand and were anxious to get off it as soon as practical. He agreed. I offered to take the lead and set a blistering pace down the glacier, in the middle of what turned out, surprisingly, to be a beautifully starry night, and was back at Camp 1 by first light around 7:00 AM. We immediately put in a radio call for an air taxi and found ourselves back in civilization at Talkeetna before 11:00 AM that morning. (Once more I got to fly out with Lowell Thomas, Jr, as our pilot. I got warmed up just talking to him about life back in Tucson.) That was quite a relief for us all. And we heard later that ours was the first and last flights off the glacier that day! We were sure thankful that we had hiked all night long to reach our base camp when we did.

The next order of business was a long overdue shower, after almost three weeks without one, and then breakfast at the Talkeetna Roadhouse. I recall being offered for breakfast: eggs, bacon, sausages, waffles, pancakes, French toast, and cereal – and ended up ordering one serving of all of those items. After breakfast I went into a small store that was handy, bought a giant bottle of Coke and a large bag of chips, along with a triple decker ice cream cone – and made my way to the other end of town to make an early reservation for dinner. I just couldn't get enough food in me!

Yes, we had missed the true mountain summit by a bit, but I soon realized that I was hooked and couldn't wait to get back home to read Chapter 2 of <u>Seven Summits</u>.

<u>Postscript:</u> Before leaving Talkeetna I learned that Lew Freedman's Mt. McKinley feature article had appeared in one of the Sunday editions of the Anchorage Daily News, as planned, while we were on the mountain, but no one had kept a copy so that I could see just what he had to say about our expedition. Once home I wrote the editor of the newspaper and he was kind enough to send me a copy of the entire newspaper edition for that day. But to my dismay, my picture did not make the final cut, my age was listed incorrectly, and my name was misspelled. So much for fame and fortune.

Aconcagua (South America)/

Popo, Ixta, Orizaba

After reading the next chapter in <u>Seven Summits</u>, I decided that my next international climbing adventure would be to attempt to climb Aconcagua, the highpoint of Argentina – as well as the highest mountain in South America – at 22,830 ft. In fact, Aconcagua is the highest mountain in the world outside of the Himalaya.

I had coerced a good friend, Steve Bridges, from Sierra Vista, Arizona, into joining me on this climb. (I only had to agree to join him on his planned climb of Mt. Kilimanjaro, the high point of Africa, sometime following this climb.)

Steve Bridges had never been to any elevation over 14,000 ft., so, as he prepared for our upcoming climb of Aconcagua, he decided that first he wanted to try his hand at something a little lower than 22,000 ft. He selected the trio of snow covered volcanoes east of Mexico City, near Puebla: Pico de Orizaba at 18,850 ft., Popocatepetl ("Popo," "The Smoking Mountain") at 17,887 ft., and Iztaccihuatl ("Ixta," "The Sleeping Woman") at 17,343 ft., the third, fifth, and seventh highest peaks in North America respectively. I decided to join him in this adventure.

So, in late November 1989, Steve and I flew to Mexico City and joined an expedition organized by the American Alpine Institute and led by Tom Dickey and Jeff Radford. While Tom had not climbed any of these three peaks previously, he had ten years of climbing experience in the Alps, South America, and the Himalaya. Jeff, on the other hand, had more than twenty five ascents of these volcanoes. Once more, we were in good hands.

After a couple days of touring around Mexico City, including visiting the famous Museum of Anthropology, our team of ten clients and two guides drove to Amecameca and on to the Tlamacas Hikers Lodge at almost 13,000 ft. elevation right on the slope of Popo. There we spent two days continuing our body's altitude acclimatization with day hikes up Popo's slopes to around 14,000 ft. On our third day there we were up at 1:30 AM and on our way up Popo by headlamp at 3:00 AM in sub-freezing temperatures and a light snowstorm – reaching the summit shortly after noon fully roped up and with ice axes and crampons. We were back at the lodge by 4 PM for a well-earned rest. All but one of the clients made the summit although some of them were very slow.

After a full day's rest, we repeated this same exercise, but this time summiting nearby Ixta before noon and back at the lodge by 3 PM. This climb wasn't nearly as demanding as Popo, but we were rewarded with an absolutely stunning view of Popo's classic cone-shaped summit at sunrise. All but three of our clients managed to reach the summit. Two down, one more to go.

We drove further east to Puebla where we treated ourselves to a day of rest – which meant good pizza and Mexican beer – and toured the impressive Cholula ruins as well as other sites which were important in Mexico's revolutionary war with Spain. Some of the original twelve clients bailed at this point and went home since they had not been feeling well all along. We did pick up a new client who appeared out of the woodwork so our team was now at two guides and seven clients.

The following day we drove to the town of Tlachichuca where we got a four-wheel drive truck and driver to haul us and our gear up the mountain to the run-down Piedra Grande Hut at about 14,000 ft. elevation. We spent two days there continuing our altitude acclimatization before heading up the mountain on our third day at 3:30 AM – reaching snow and ice in an hour, Orizaba's crater rim before 10:00 AM and at the rim's highpoint shorty after that. The descent back to the hut, the truck back to Tlachichuca, and a drive back to Pueblo for the night went by quickly. We were elated that we had gotten all three of these summits in such a straightforward manner without any problems with weather, health, or stamina. We decided that we were now ready for Argentina's Aconcagua.

We were still on a climber's high as we flew out of Tucson at the tail end of December 1989 headed for Mendoza, Argentina, for a go at the mighty Aconcagua. While Aconcagua is substantially higher than any others we've been up, all of the route descriptions for the popular "Normal" Horcones Valley route, via the Plaza de Mulas base camp, describes it as being very straightforward in good weather. In fact, the relatively easy access route often lures climbers into climbing high too soon and too fast before first achieving effective altitude acclimatization – leading to seriously dangerous consequences when the body revolts.

Our guide for this climb, arranged once more by Genet Expeditions, was to be John Schwieder who I had met on Mt. McKinley in April 1987 – with Daniel Burrieza, an Argentine native, as our Base Camp manager. (Daniel has run 40 expeditions on this mountain, including 24 summit ascents, so we are, once more, in good hands.)

Joining Steve and me on this expedition were Joe and Linda Dalmas, good friends and workmates at IBM Tucson, together with five others.

After a night of serious New Year's Eve celebrating and the next day recovering (and a review of all of our personal gear), we were bused to the Puenta del Inca lodge for the night - very close to the Chilean border at around 8,000 ft. elevation. Here we had our first views up the Horcones Valley, where we would be hiking, as well as the summit of Aconcagua itself. That next morning ten mules arrived - together with several gauchos (Argentinian cowboys) – to haul our packs and gear to Plaza de Mulas that would be our base camp for the expedition. We were told that each mule could handle a load of 60 kilograms – or about 130 lbs. We would be hiking with only a day pack which was welcome.

We used two days to reach our base camp – wading across the frigid Horcones River up to our waists at one point. That first night we slept out in the meadow on the grass enjoying the constellations in the southern hemisphere – including my very first view of the Southern Cross constellation.

The Plaza de Mulas base camp, at about 14,000 ft. elevation, was a real zoo with almost 100 tents jammed into a very small area – with climbing groups from Australia, Yugoslavia, Argentina, Chile, USA,

Japan, Switzerland, Germany, Spain, France, and England among others. It certainly had an international flavor!

Our plan called for us to rest here at base camp for two days before carrying a load up to our next camp, Camp 1, Nido de Condores ("Nest of the Condors") at around 17,900 ft. elevation. Since I was feeling fine, I immediately loaded up my daypack with my camera, a sweater, and some water, and casually headed up the access trail for a three hour hike – reaching 17,000 ft. elevation, within sight of our next camp, with no altitude issues at all – and was back down to base camp in about an hour – still feeling great. I was jazzed and ready for this peak.

At dinner Daniel announced that our route to the summit was very dry – with no ice at all and only occasional small patches of snow. That means that we won't need our crampons, ice axes, ropes or harnesses. That was welcome news. But he also reminded us that we would be ascending the highest peak in the world outside of the Himalaya and, therefore, it needed to be treated with all due respect.

After a second day of rest and acclimatization at base camp, we loaded up for a carry up to Camp 1. The weather was holding just fine: sub-freezing temps at night with shirtsleeve temps in mid-day – with clear skies. We all carried food, stoves, and fuel up the mountain. Steve and I were the first to reach Camp 1 with our loads in less than four hours – a half hour ahead of John - and over an hour ahead of the others – with no headaches or other altitude problems. Karen was experiencing symptoms of AMS (acute mountain sickness) and couldn't make it beyond 17,000 ft. The others were suffering splitting headaches – with plenty of foot blisters on the descent back to base camp. Overall, this was not a good sign for the group. Several of the clients claim to have climbed Mt. McKinley and several others to have climbed Mt. Kilimanjaro, but the fitness that this implies was not evident here.

We took an additional rest day at base camp.

The next day Karen's symptoms had progressed to those of HAPE (high altitude pulmonary edema), which is very serious, and so she was med-evac'd out on a helicopter that had been summoned to evacuate another climber who had succumbed to altitude much higher up the mountain.

We came to understand that, year-to-date, there had already been five rescues on the mountain – though no deaths so far.

The following day we loaded up and carried up to Camp 1. Steve and I were again the first to reach our campsite with Russ only a half hour later. The rest of the group was a full hour later than us. Fortunately, Steve, Russ and I had parts to our common tent, so we could set it up, anchor it down securely with rocks, and get out of the cold wind. It was 32° F outside with increasing winds while inside it was a comfortable 60° F. Later we went back outside to build a rock wall of sorts around the tent to provide further wind protection. There was a good source of water at a small lake only a couple hundred yards away.

Our plan called for us to take a rest day here at Camp 1 – which meant that we'd take a leisurely afternoon stroll, with day packs, up to our next and final camp, the famous Berlin Camp, at 19,200 ft. elevation. All the while we could easily see the summit, another almost 4,000 ft. above us – and the infamous Canaleta, a steep scree slope made up of small, very loose rocks leading directly to the summit. Daniel had told us that this final slope to the summit was the crux of the whole climb – requiring as much time, energy, and perseverance to complete as was the entire rest of the climb to that point.

We came to understand that Steve Bridges, Russ and I were often referred to as the "old guys" since we were all over 40 while we got to referring to the other three climbers, Ross, Steve Van Nuys, and Greg, as the "kids" since they were all under 30. I guess Joe and Linda were in a class by themselves – sometimes being referred to as the "newlyweds" though they had been married for many years. Joe had been suffering from a chest cold this past week, but was beginning to recover and was looking forward to his summit bid. Unfortunately, he appeared to have handed off the cold to Linda.

The next day, on plan, we loaded up and hiked up to the Berlin Camp – again setting up our tents and securing them as best we could in the rocks. Once more the "old guys" reached Berlin Camp a full hour and a half ahead of the "kids."

To that point our weather had been excellent, but that was changing.

High winds were building - together with some snow – causing us to hunker down inside our tents to sit it out. Shades of Mt. McKinley? This I knew how to do, from my McKinley experience, but I sure wasn't looking forward to it.

Early that evening John came by each tent with a serving of some sort of unappetizing looking instant pasta for our dinner menu, but none of us had any taste for that – or anything else for that matter. A short while later he came by again to apologize for the dinner saying that he had prepared it incorrectly and asked us not to eat it. We gave it back – gladly – untouched. And within another hour he returned with more instant pasta, prepared correctly this time, but not looking any more appetizing. We had a Clif bar instead and tried to sleep.

That night the winds really built up – sounding like a freight train was passing by our tent. It was scary, but the tents held up well. These winds continued all through the next day and into that night, too, making us wonder if we'd ever get a shot at the summit.

The following morning the winds had let up a bit and John was betting on it totally quieting down and so he asked us to prepare for a summit bid. He counted noses and found interest from Steve Bridges, Joe and me with all of the others opting to go back down to base camp at their first opportunity. Russ opted out simply because he thought that our chances of actually summiting were too slim given the weather conditions. Linda was suffering from the chest cold that she got from Joe. But what we didn't learn until several days later was that "the kids" were told that they could join the summit team only if they were sure that they could keep up with the "old guys," since, with only one leader, we couldn't split into two separate climbing teams, and they already knew that they weren't fit enough to do that. It was a compact, but committed summit team for sure. We didn't actually leave Berlin Camp until after 11 AM and were at the base of the feared Canaleta by shortly after 3 PM. Joe and John were on top in two hours with Steve and me another 45 minutes behind that. We were very excited to have finally made the top. After the required photos and back slapping, we high-tailed it back to Berlin Camp and were there in less than two hours – totally wasted, but exhilarated with our success. For those few moments on top we four were the highest people in the entire world!

That next morning, after having slept like a rock all night, we packed up and hiked back to base camp, a descent of some 5,000 ft. in about three hours. We must have passed fifty hikers heading up the trail as we were descending. This mountain was remaining popular.

The following morning, after an excellent breakfast, we packed up everything and hiked back out to Puenta del Inca in eight and a half hours. We showered, dined, and got bused back to civilization in Mendoza that same evening and a day later were in the air flying back to the US.

One more successful summit. We were elated. Kilimanjaro here we come!

Postscript: Russ Patrick, one of the "old guys" who shared the tent with Steve and me at Nido de Condores and at Berlin Camp, had kept a very complete diary of his summit effort throughout his entire trip. And, to our surprise, he got it published, word for word, in the Los Angeles Times in January 1991. We were all anxious to read it to get his impression of all of us and our summit effort.

Kilimanjaro (Africa)

The next continental highpoint turned out to be very straightforward –
especially when compared with Mt. McKinley and Aconcagua. Everyone
has heard of Kilimanjaro, at 19,340 ft., even if one doesn't know that it
is in Tanzania, or doesn't quite remember exactly where Tanzania is on
the continent of Africa. Tanzanians like to tell people that, if measured
from the center of the earth, Kilimanjaro is even taller than Mt. Everest
– this due to the Earth not being really round, but rather seriously bulged
out around its midriff - and Kilimanjaro being located very close to the
equator. (Of course, Ecuador, located also on the equator, makes the same
claim about its own Mt. Chimborazo at 20,703 ft.)

Completing my commitment to Steve Bridges to climb Kilimanjaro
with him, following his agreement to tackle Aconcagua with me, I found
myself packing and flying to the Kilimanjaro Airport in Arusha, Tanzania,
on the first of July 1990, just six months after summiting Aconcagua in
Argentina. This was going to be a challenge to both my bankroll as well
as my vacation budget. I would have preferred to have delayed that trip
until I had earned a little more vacation time at work, but a promise is a
promise, and Steve had already committed to join Sobek Expeditions for
their trip at this time.

My flight to Tanzania turned out to have been really international what
with flight stops in New York, London, Rome and Addis Ababa, Ethiopia,
before landing in Tanzania. We were relieved at being told in route that the
pilot was going to skip a planned stop at the Entebbe Airport in Uganda. A
very recent night time commando raid by Israel on this airport (in order to
free up some kidnapped Israelis being held there) rather soured relations
between Uganda's unpredictable president and the West.

Based on everything that I had read about climbing Kilimanjaro, there
were two "secrets" to a successful climb: arrive fit and climb slow.

Sobek took care of the second requirement to "climb slow" by carefully
laying out a staged assault on the mountain. We were scheduled to use

five days to ascend from the Machame entrance gate at around 6,000 ft. to the Barafu Hut camp at about 15,000 ft., our high camp, or about an 1800 ft. /day average – with about 5 – 7 hours of hiking per day. That sounded very reasonable to me.

Our climbing group consisted of our guide, Conrad Hirsch, an experienced whitewater rafting guide, and 16 clients. And each client had his own personal porter to carry his tent and backpack so that we would only be carrying daypacks with water, rain gear, camera, and a sweater or jacket. In addition, we had "food porters" carrying all of our meal provisions for the week – including dishes, pots, and utensils. The porters were mostly from the local Chuga tribe who live in one of two villages in the foothills at the base of Kilimanjaro.

Some of us squeezed in a short day hike two days in a row, around the base of Kilimanjaro, as we waited for the rest of the clients to show up. But since we were in a rainforest, we weren't surprised to have it rain on us. On one hike to a waterfall, I spied what I was sure was Arizona cypress, variegated agave, and a form of Organ Pipe cactus – which made it feel a bit like home.

On that first climbing day, after turning over our backpacks to the porters at the Machame Gate, we didn't get off until 1:30 PM, but still reached our first tent camp, in the rain, still in the rain forest, before 6 PM. It got down to freezing that night and was very misty and rainy through that following morning, but by late afternoon of that second day we were above the rain clouds, out of the rain forest, hiking now in heather, under a warm sun and blue sky, and got our first views of Kilimanjaro's snow-covered summit. That was inspiring. But clearly the real highlight of the day was having gotten delivered hot tea at our tents as part of our morning wake up call. We also got a bowl of warm water with which to wash up a bit. We could quickly get used to that kind of service!

This routine continued for three more days – slowly ascending the mountain – in stable weather and excellent views of nearby mountains – finally reaching our high camp at 15,000 ft. We lost one client on our second day (out of the total group of 16 clients). He had been hiking very slowly and said that he wasn't feeling well. But he also admitted that he had not managed to give up his smoking habit as he had promised his partner. So he was escorted back down the mountain by his porter where he could arrange for a lift back to town. (Interestingly, his partner also bailed out – but this time within a couple hours of the summit. He admitted to having just given up smoking, but had never gotten really serious about physical training.)

We did see plenty of old panther sign along the way up the mountain, but the only real wildlife that we saw was a duiker – a very small antelope – and he was making tracks to get as far away from us as he could.

That night we were out of our tents and on the trail, by plan, at 1:15 AM – heading for the crater rim – reaching it by 7:30 AM – and reaching the crater rim's highpoint, Uhuru Point, in less than an hour after that. The trail from camp was steep and rocky up to the rim, while the trail along the rim was covered in well packed snow. With the moon out full all night long, we didn't even need to use our headlamps to see the route. We had fourteen folks all totally tickled with themselves that they had successfully summited Kili and that everything after that would be downhill.

After all of the mandatory summit photos, we hiked back along the crater rim to Gilman Point, down to the Kibo Hut, and then another 8 miles down to the Horombo Hut where we stayed the night in some bunk houses. In the morning we continued our descent to the Marangu Gate – reaching it by 2:00 PM. From there we got a lift to a hotel in Marangu for a well-earned hot shower. The last day saw us returning to Arusha for some tourist shopping and a farewell dinner before heading home. One more continental highpoint checked off the list.

Post Script: In 2003 my son, Scott, invited me to join him for his climb of Kilimanjaro. I couldn't pass up the opportunity to share that climb with him – and especially so since it was his intent to follow up the climb with several days on a safari out on the famous Serengeti Game Reserve – an opportunity that I missed out on for my 1990 Kilimanjaro climb.

This expedition was organized by Mountain Madness, an American mountain guide service that had been run by Scott Fisher until his untimely death in the famous Mt. Everest tragedy of 1996. We had only seven clients for this climb ranging in age from a 17 year old high school student with absolutely no prior climbing experience up to a 50 year old dentist who, in years past, had climbed Aconcagua, Orizaba, and Mt. Blanc, and had been to the Everest base camp – and Scott and me.

Our trip leader, Ben, was a native Masai who seemed to be known by every African in Tanzania! He had extensive training in mountaineering and mountain medicine, most of it in the US, and was EMT qualified. His hand-selected porter and kitchen staff numbered 55! So, we were quite the entourage moving up the mountain together.

Before tackling the mountain we spent a couple of orientation days at a special wilderness tent camp in the nearby rain forest of Arusha National Park where, on a guided hike, we saw giraffes, warthogs, baboons, cape buffalo, and four different species of antelope. That served as a nice introduction to our upcoming safari expedition following our climb.

Once more we moved up the mountain very slowly, giving our bodies time to acclimate to the increasing elevation. We used six camps from the start of our trail up to our final high camp, via the Breach Wall – this time inside Kili's crater at 19,000 ft. - for a climbing pace of about 1,700 ft./day. On each one of these climbing days we managed to reach our next higher camp by noon giving us every afternoon off for a nap and a day hike in the area.

One highlight of this ascent was at Lava Camp at 14,500 ft. on Christmas Eve where we celebrated with a mess tent decorated with tinsel, candles, favors, Christmas gifts for everyone, cake, champagne, plus a whole ham that had been cooking all of that afternoon in a special pressure cooker brought along just for that purpose. Then, following dinner, the porters serenaded us with Christmas carols, the Tanzanian national anthem, and other seasonal songs – followed by a special Masai native dance routine that included a lot of high jumping in place. It was great fun for one and all.

Our high camp inside the crater was immediately below the rim's Uhuru

Point – the mountain's highpoint – so our scramble to the summit that next morning was measured in minutes and not hours. Once we left our camp, Scott and I were on top in a little over 30 minutes with the rest of our group arriving shortly after that.

Our many porters, of course, had no need to follow us up to the summit choosing instead a short cut across the crater floor to our descent route. However, I did finally notice that one porter followed us up to the summit. And, in fact, he had been following us close at hand all week long. Only then did I figure out that he was carrying in his pack a complete medical kit, emergency oxygen, and a Gamow bag for any medical emergency that might occur. I was impressed. (A Gamow bag was invented by a Russian doctor of that name. It is a zippered, rubberized fabric bag big enough to house a patient suffering from serious altitude illness. It can be pressurized with a foot pump to simulate the air pressure found at lower elevations giving the patient temporary relief from any altitude health issues.)

Scott was particularly impressed when Ben took an incoming call on his cell phone from the Mountain Madness home office in Seattle, Washington, asking us how we were doing. Scott said that that was far better cell coverage than he had back home in the technology capital of San Jose, California! After celebrating our summit success with a zillion photographs, we descended via the Machame / Mweki Route and were at our camp for the night on the edge of the rain forest at about 10,000 ft. in only four hours – a descent of 9,000 ft. We were smokin'! Now we could celebrate in comfort because now the air was thick and we could breathe again.

The following morning we hiked easily the final two hours to the Mweka entrance gate for lunch and a quick drive back to the Moivara Lodge in Arusha. The next day, while the rest packed to go home, Scott and I and two others from our group flew out to Seronera in the Serengeti National Park to begin our safari tour. The famous wildebeest migration was well underway and herds of them were visible from the air by the tens of thousands – maybe hundreds of thousands. By evening we had spotted and identified some 22 different mammals, including zebras, hippos, hyenas, giraffes, elephants, crocodiles, a spotted leopard, and seven different species of antelope. We also identified 14 different species of large birds. What a treat!

We spent the night in a tent camp within a copse of tall trees out on the Serengeti plains – with a lioness with cubs for company. The next day our animal sightings increased to include lions, a cheetah, baboons, monkeys, ostriches, mongoose, cape buffalo, a jackal, among others, together with many more bird species.

From there we drove by the famous Oldavai Gorge where the Leakeys had first discovered evidence of humans from almost 3 million years ago, and then on to the Ngorongoro Crater where we saw even more wildlife including black rhinos and a serval cat. That evening we celebrated New Years with cake and champagne following a dinner of freshly slaughtered goat. Along the way Scott and I both managed to purchase our very own official six foot long Masai spears though we had yet to figure out how we were going to get them home. We were disappointed that they didn't come with an instruction manual.

Following a relaxing rest day at the Moivaro Lodge back in Arusha, we caught a shuttle bus to Nairobi, Kenya, for our flights home.

Mt. Elbrus (Europe)

Mt. Elbrus, at 18,481 ft., is almost totally unknown to everyone – including many mountain climbers. Ask about the highest mountain in Europe and most people think only of Western Europe and its Mt. Blanc located in the Alps on the French-Italian border at 15,771 ft. But our junior high school geography class taught us that the continent of Europe extends well into Russia as far east as the Ural Mountains. With that in mind it is a little easier to accept that continental Europe's highpoint is in the Caucasus Mountains on the border between Russia and the Republic of Georgia. (Interestingly, this mountain range also includes Europe's second, third, and fourth highest peaks.) And since I had already completed climbs on three continental high points, it seemed natural to make Europe's continental highest my next goal. So in August 1991 I was on my way to Russia's Mt. Elbrus on an expedition arranged by Mountain Travel-Sobek and led by a Mexican-American by the name of Sergio Fitch-Watkins. Sixteen clients signed up for this climb: 15 from the US and one from Switzerland – aged from 23 to 61. (The 61 year old was a fire hydrant salesman from Tucson.)

And our trip was interesting right from the start. I flew to New York and on to Helsinki, Finland, where I transferred to a Russian TU-154 flown by Russia's Aeroflot Airlines – which, next to China Air, had the worst reputation for flight safety in the world. And I got my chance to experience that on my very first flight with them. The sky was totally socked in as we approached the Moscow Airport – descending through heavy cloud cover. When we finally broke out of the clouds and could see the ground, I saw that we were actually flying <u>below</u> the tops of the nearby trees just off our wing tips! The pilot, realizing this at least as quickly as I did, immediately pulled up the flaps, gunned the engines, and fought for elevation – back into the clouds. After another 10 – 15 minutes we again descended – this time onto the airport runway. What a relief!

After a quick dinner and a night of rest in the Moscow Hotel, we walked one block to the famous Red Square, Lenin's Tomb, St. Basil's Cathedral, the famous GUM department store, and the dreaded Kremlin – home of the Soviet Union's government. That afternoon we sat in on a formal street play with a medieval theme, but replete with more modern themes of labor vs government political issues – a thinly disguised form of political protest.

We also saw evidence of America's first commercial inroad into the Soviet consumer economy exhibited by the country's very first McDonalds, Pizza Hut, and Baskin Robbins restaurants. Interestingly, when we checked out the McDonalds restaurant, which had a line out front waiting for service that was over two blocks long, we discovered that foreigners, because they had hard currency, had their own special entrance and were waited on almost immediately. The Moscow city restaurants had very extensive menus, but seldom had more than one or two of those items actually available to their customers. The consumer supply system was in tatters.

That next day, after waiting around for over eight hours, we finally got loaded onto our plane at Moscow's domestic airport for an in-country flight south to Mineralye Vody – near the southern border of Russia. The departure airport did pass our entire luggage through their standard x-ray machines, but I couldn't help but notice that these machines weren't even plugged in and no one was actually looking at the x-ray's display screen! Some security control! None of us got actual boarding passes, but, again, because we paid for our tickets with hard currency, we got to board first – choosing whatever seat that we wanted. Then the masses were released to load in one mad rush. Stewardesses were available during loading, but I was never quite sure what their jobs were exactly, since I never saw them actually doing anything. And they totally disappeared once the plane took off – never to be seen from again until after landing. Using seatbelts appeared to only be a suggestion since no one checked to see if we were using them – and most people did not. Upon landing, followed by a four hour bus ride, we reached a very fancy dacha, much like a classy Swiss chalet, at 6,000 ft. elevation - that was usually reserved for the Communist Party's elite. That would be our home when we were not on the mountain.

That next morning we went for our first acclimatization hike up the Usangi Valley to about 8,500 ft. elevation – followed by lunch at 4:00

and dinner at 8:00 PM back at the dacha. We repeated this exercise our second morning, but now reaching 12,000 ft. elevation – with the help of two chair lifts. From here we had excellent views of the twin-summited Mt. Elbrus and the whole Baksan Valley.

On the walk back to the dacha I asked Sergio whether he had sized up the group yet and what he could expect on summit day. He said that he was predicting that five would be on the 'A' Team to be guided up the West Summit and five would be on the 'B' Team to be guided up the East Summit. When I asked him about the rest, he said that they will eventually discover that they have paid a lot of money to take a long, hard uphill walk in the snow since that's all that they have conditioned themselves for.

Our third day here had us packing up and heading up to the famous Priutt Hut on the slopes of Mt. Elbrus at 13,800 ft. elevation via two gondola lifts, a chair lift, and a two hour hike in soft snow. It had been raining all night long and continued into the day – turning to snow as we approached the Priutt Hut – in high winds. The Priutt Hut is a huge, metal-clad building looking much like a gigantic Airstream Trailer that had bunk room and dining area space for more than 100 climbers at a time. And with the lousy weather outside, we were glad to be inside.

On our fourth day here we day-hiked with our crampons and ice axes in improving weather to an obvious band of rocks on steep terrain up to about 15,500 ft. Six of our team could not make it that far.

On our fifth day, our summit day, we were up at 1:45 AM, breakfast at 2:00 AM, and on the trail with headlamps by 3:00 AM – organized into three rope teams of 5, 5, and 6 with a guide for each group. My rope team, the A Team, led by Alec, a Russian guide, reached the rock band by 5:00 AM, just as the first rays of sunrise were visible, and into the saddle between the two summits by 8:00 AM – almost an hour ahead of the B Team. Feeling a bit under the weather, I and one other climber rested, while the A Team went for the West Summit. Soon we joined the B Team, led by Sergio, and went to the East Summit – reaching it by 11:00 AM. We were back at the Priutt Hut by 2:00 PM in an easy three hours. As predicted, the C Team folks had a nice morning walk on the mountain before returning to the hut.

That evening in the hut we started hearing stories that there had been a major coup in Moscow, but we didn't give it much notice since we were exhausted and still basking in the glory of our summit success.

In the morning we were quickly back to the gondolas, down the rest of the mountain, bused to the dacha, savoring a hot shower, and enjoying wine and vodka. Once there we could no longer avoid the fact that, while we were on the mountain, something of serious political significance had occurred back in Moscow. But it wasn't until we could round up some local resident with radio access to BBC that we learned anything more. The local TV station was playing the Swan Lake Opera over and over again in lieu of offering any real news.

We eventually discovered that the president of the Soviet Union, Mikhail Gorbachev, had been kidnapped, somewhere in Ukraine, and was being held hostage. A 12-man government committee had declared themselves to be in charge of the government. The Soviet Army had been called out to take positions in Moscow and Petersburg and the people were rioting. The airlines were shut down stranding us, at least temporarily, in our dacha. We began looking at maps to try to ferret out a way to escape into Georgia from which we could, perhaps, make it to Turkey and home. We busied ourselves for the next two days with day hikes in the area and then, on the third day, we heard that the coup was over, Gorbachev was released, the airlines were running again, and so we were soon headed back to the airport at Mineralye Vody and caught the first flight back to Moscow.

What we had missed was that while we were out of touch with the outside world, Boris Yeltsin, the president of Russia, had made a major speech on the steps of the Russian Parliament Building, during all of the rioting, declaring that the committee of 12, who claimed to be in charge of the U.S.S.R, had no legal standing and should release President Gorbachev, return him back to power, and send the soldiers back to their bases. There were surely other factors involved here, too, but we were ignorant of them and, in any case, it worked. By the time we made it back to Moscow, the soldiers had all retreated, the rioting ceased, and mourning was underway for the few patriots that had died in the skirmishes with the army. The streets were still littered with rocks, burnt buses, and other riot debris. And the citizenry was wandering around trying to figure out the significance of what had just occurred. Such a relatively peaceful protest had never occurred before. What we did see, though, was that in the process, all of the classic Soviet Union hammer and sickle flags on all of the buildings had been quietly replaced with the red, blue and white Russian flag. Interestingly, by the end of the year, the Soviet Union had totally dissolved as most all of the previous Soviet republics had declared their independence from the USSR. And Gorbachev was out of a job.

We helped the Russians celebrate that evening in a local restaurant with lots of vodka and far too many toasts to Gorbachev. The next morning several of us stumbled our way onto a plane out of Moscow and on to Petersburg, formerly Lenningrad, for some more traditional sightseeing. Over the next three days we visited all of the traditional tourist stops, including the Hermitage, the summer palace, churches, museums, and a boat tour on the Neva River before taking the train to Helsinki, Finland, for our flight home. I was especially impressed with our tour of the Hermitage, once the winter home of the czars, and now the largest art museum in the Soviet Union – holding some 3 million works of art and culture. Not able to see anywhere near all of it on a brief hour and a half tour, we were invited, at the end of our first hour, to select one era of art to focus on for the balance of our time there. Speaking for our whole tour group, I selected French Impressionism and our guide applauded my choice. We then spent the next half hour touring through rooms and rooms full of art by Cezanne, Picasso, Raphael, van Gogh, Monet, Degas, Gauguin, and Renoir among others. This made a special impression on me because these pieces of art had not been handed down from the czars, since the revolution had taken place well before this art era, but rather had been purchased by the Soviet Communist Committee for the appreciation by the masses.

A fun little vignette: As we were finishing our tour of the famous Summer Palace of Peter the Great, just outside of Petersburg, I noticed that our tour guide was leafing through a translated copy of The Life and Times of Thomas Jefferson, a recent best seller in the US. I asked her if she knew who Thomas Jefferson was, and she responded that she thought that he had been a US president at one point, but didn't know anything further. Remembering that our former President John Kennedy had been well known and liked in Russia, I offered her a story about Kennedy that referred to Jefferson. That perked her ears. I then related that at one point during the Kennedy administration, Jackie Kennedy had planned a massive evening dinner in the White House where she had invited all of the culturally notable celebrities in the US. Upon entering this room full of dignitaries, the president was heard to say, "There is more intelligence and culture collected here this evening than at any other time in the history of the White House - save for when Thomas Jefferson dined here alone." Our tour guide immediately picked up the book and headed for the cashier!

Postscript: While saying our goodbyes in Moscow to Sergio, our trip leader, he took me aside to explain that he had just received approval from the Nepalese government to lead a climb of Mt. Everest that next spring and was offering me a spot on his team - for only $15,000 (plus, maybe, an additional $700 for oxygen). I was floored since the going rate at the time for a spot on an Everest climbing team was $65,000. It still would require almost three months of time off work and so, after stewing on it for quite a while, I eventually turned down the offer.

Carstensz Pyramid (Australasia)

The next continental highpoint presented an interesting choice. The highpoint of the continent of Australia is the well-known Mt. Kosciusko, just outside of Sydney, in southeastern Australia. But at only 7,310 ft. in elevation, it is hardly worth an expensive and time-consuming flight there and back without some other excuse to visit. In fact, I have some good friends who have hiked this peak in tennis shoes and a picnic basket. It's certainly not a serious mountaineering challenge.

So I decided to expand my definition of the continent of Australia to include the entire continental plate of Australia. Now we can consider places like New Zealand, (which does have Mt. Cook, a serious snow-covered mountain), Tasmania, Sumatra, and mountainous West and East New Guinea. When these are considered, then the award-winning highpoint is clearly Carstensz Pyramid in West New Guinea (also known as Irian Jaya or Papua by the Indonesians) at 16,023 ft. – named after a Dutch sea captain who, on an especially clear day, claimed that he spied snow on its summit from his ship at sea.

Many years later an Austrian adventurer by the name of Heinreich Harrer was the first westerner to penetrate the jungles of West New Guinea in 1962 for the purpose of climbing Carstensz Pyramid. Harrer already had established a reputation as an adventurer for having been on the first team to successfully scale the famous north face of the Eiger in Switzerland in 1938, described in his book, "The White Spider," and author and principal character in the book, "Seven Years in Tibet," where he hob-knobbed with the highly revered Dalai Lama in Lhasa, Tibet, for seven years while he sat out World War II. He documented his ascent of Carstensz Pyramid in his book, "I Came from the Stone Age" detailing not only the climb itself, but also his encounters with the Dani people in and around Carstensz. Seeing that they truly were still living in the Stone Age, he hired a bunch of them to escort him to the base of Carstensz Pyramid by paying them with steel axe heads.

Of course, I soon discovered that I was not the first person to figure out the significance of Carstensz Pyramid. But I was tickled to discover that Alpine Ascents International (AAI), an American-based mountain guiding service, was running a commercial trip to climb it and I immediately signed up to join them.

When I talked once more with my friend Steve Bridges to see if he would be interested in joining me on such a trip, he asked me what I knew about the area. I told him truthfully that all I knew about the area was that the mountain was in a tropical rain forest, 3 degrees off the equator, where it rains nearly every day, often all day long, it was reported to be surrounded by cannibals, and that he should sign up immediately! He did!

Our first trip plan with AAI for 1992 fell through when the Indonesian government cancelled our climbing permit – without explanation. But AAI applied again two years later and were quickly approved. So, in January 1994, we were off to West New Guinea with a team of 6 clients. Our two guides, Todd Burleson, owner of Alpine Ascents, and Pete Athans, a three time Mt. Everest summiteer, put us in good hands. A third mountain guide, Henry Todd, from Scotland, was along to learn the ropes of leading a climb up Carstensz.

Getting there became the next challenge. We signed up for a commercial flight from Los Angeles to Jakarta, Indonesia, with a refueling stop on the tiny Pacific island of Biak – just north of the coast of West New Guinea. We wrangled a way to get off the plane in Biak, along with our luggage, and quickly contracted with a private air service to shuttle us on one of their twin props from Biak to the city of Nabiri on the northern coast of West New Guinea. From there we contracted with a second air service to shuttle us the next day into the interior to a tiny village called Ilaga populated by the very primitive Dani people. We landed on the only semi-flat land around – an old sweet potato patch at the edge of their village at an elevation of about 7,200 ft.

We were quickly met there by some 40 - 50 naked, fierce-looking Dani men wearing nothing but penis gourds and bones in their noses. The women, in their short, reed grass skirts, were almost as skimpily clad. The men helped carry our gear to the village proper, about a mile away. What an exotic spectacle that was!!

We were joined there by two Indonesian mountaineering guides, Ripto and Ogun, who were to be our interpreters. Unfortunately, they didn't speak any of the native Dani tongue and very little English either. Things got more interesting from there.

Also stationed in Ilaga was a detachment of trigger-happy Indonesian soldiers who immediately confiscated all of our passports – promising to return them when we returned to Ilaga after our climb.

Negotiations began that next morning to hire some of these natives to help us carry our gear and show us the way through the jungle to the base of Carstensz – an estimated 55 km away as the crow flies. Once determining how much weight each could (or would) carry, around 35 lbs., we calculated that we would need around 30 - 35 people to act as guide-porters. The selection process started with a short PT test to be sure that those offering their services were physically capable.

Our next surprise was in discovering that we needed to provide food for all of these porters for the duration of the trip – which was expected to be at least five days out, five days back, and several days at the mountain base itself. The main staple of the Dani people was sweet potatoes and so off to the Ilaga village center to purchase one really huge pile of sweet potatoes. These were quickly divided into individual carry loads which meant hiring a bunch more porters to carry these sweet potatoes – and then – you guessed it – buying more sweet potatoes to feed these sweet potato-carrying porters – and then........well, you get the idea. When we were finally ready to leave the village the next day, as soon as the Dani chief gave his approval, we were to be escorted by some 75 Dani natives carrying our gear and lots and lots of sweet potatoes!

They all showed up the next morning, with the chief's approval, for the start of our long walk – armed with bows and arrows and knives – all crudely made from various jungle woods, fibers, bones, and other materials. As if we needed more evidence of the primitive nature of these tribesmen, we couldn't help but notice that their understanding of archery had not yet advanced to the point where they saw the benefit of putting fletching ("feathers") on the ends of their arrows to help them fly straight. As a result, while they appeared to be deadly accurate at very close range, their arrows just diverged wildly at any moderate distance.

Most of the "labor negotiations" were conducted between Ogun, our Indonesian guide, and one Dani serving as something of a work foreman, so it was not easy to learn what the porters were being paid for their labor, but I did witness them all getting issued a package of saltpeter, a package of loose tobacco, and a package of cigarette paper at the trip start. Most of them turned over the saltpeter to their wives suggesting that it would get used as a meat preservative, but that's only a guess. They certainly owned no firearms, so we ruled out them using it to manufacture gun powder.

Without detailed maps of the area, or the use of modern GPS's, it was very difficult to figure out how far we travelled each day, but it was probably less than ten miles since the terrain was very hilly and the trail very steep and muddy and wet – and it was either raining hard or getting ready to do so most of the time.

Day 1: That first day on the trail we stopped around 3 PM to make camp at about 9,500 ft. elevation. We were in lightweight nylon tents, but set up a variety of large tarps to cook under and to shelter the Dani. They huddled around smoky fires at night under these tarps. It rained all night long.

Day 2: We were back on the trail by 7:45 AM in welcome sunshine, which helped our demeanor, but the rains returned by 9 AM and lasted all day long. We did manage to break out of the rain forest proper around noon, at about 11,500 ft. elevation, and into a rolling savanna – stopping to make camp around 2 PM – in the rain – which continued until midnight.

Here I got a quick lesson in Dani-style community property. Several of us had had the foresight to purchase umbrellas back at the seashore town of Nabiri – never imagining just how useful they would be on the trail. But, once on the trail, when I had occasion to put mine down to take a photograph or retrieve something from my pack, it was a signal to the Dani that I no longer needed it – permitting one of them to pick it up and begin using it. Asking for it back, since it was mine, got me only a fierce look, and so my only recourse was to trail after the culprit and wait for him to put it down – at which time I could snag it back and move on – quickly.

Day 3: Up at 6 AM, on the trail by 8 AM to sunny skies, and then, you guessed it, more rain – heavy – nearly the whole day long. We made camp at 5 PM on an open plateau at about 11,800 ft. elevation.

Day 4: Up at 6 AM and on the trail by 7:30 AM with cold wind and misty weather until noon when it cleared up and was just - cold - and windy – but no rain for a change. We passed quickly by a grave site marking the spot where our Dani tribesman had fought a short battle with a warring neighbor tribe back in 1987 – resulting in the death of a young Indonesian boy - on a trekking expedition. We now understood why our Dani porters were so carefully armed. Now it was our turn to feel "naked" since none of us were armed! At our lunch stop that day the Dani set up a defensive perimeter around us while we ate. While we did walk through one abandoned Dani mountain village, we never saw any other natives on our trip.

Day 5: We finally had our first glimpse, under blue skies, of the snow-covered mountain range that included Carstensz Pyramid. This was another hard day of up and down hiking across a steep ridge – all with views of New Zealand Pass – our last major landmark (and obstacle) before reaching our Base Camp area.

At one point we had to cross a narrow, but quite deep river. Steve and I managed, with a running start, to jump across it after having tossed our day packs over first. But we soon came to realize that the Dani – not especially adept at running and jumping – were terrified of this river since none of them could swim. We endeared ourselves to them when we helped them get their loads and themselves safely across – especially those carrying our packs.

Later that afternoon one of the Dani managed to spot and kill a strange, furry mammal which they called a "cuscus." They were all delighted because they could now look forward to having a little meat with their sweet potatoes that night. This "cuscus" critter, actually a relatively rare, long-beaked echidna, looked a bit like a giant possum, complete with silky-soft, dark brown fur – which was embedded with dozens of very sharp porcupine-like quills. It was a very curious animal indeed – and certainly a first for all of us.

Day 6: Now the plan was to get as close as practical to the New Zealand Pass today so that, with any luck, we could get up and through the pass and on to our base camp in good weather tomorrow since, at 14,000 ft. elevation, the pass would be too cold and snowy for the scantily-clad porters to travel through in a storm. We achieved our objective and had camp established by noon just below the pass at about 12,400 ft. elevation, but it had been hard climbing up the very steep and muddy trail. Rain started again at sundown and rained all night long.

Day 7: Awoke to heavy rain – what else? – and the porters didn't want to move. The rain didn't stop, but it did let up a bit around 10:00 AM and we convinced the porters to give it a try since we couldn't see any fresh snow in the pass. We managed to make it up and over the pass and on to the base camp area at about 13,000 ft. elevation, well above timberline, by 2:00 PM with surprisingly little snow in the pass or in camp. But everything was soaked – of course. And the wind was very cold. All around us were sharp, rocky ridges. Welcome to the mountains! And off in the far distance was Freeport-McMoRan's huge Grasberg copper and gold mine. We decided right then and there to take a shot at the summit at first light in the morning and immediately started breaking out our ropes, harnesses, and other climbing gear in order to be ready. We had to complete the ascent and descent in a single day because there just wasn't any place along the way to use for an interim overnight camp.

Day 8: We were up at 4:00 AM to broken skies and on the trail by 5:00 AM for the one hour hike, by headlamps and moonlight, to the bottom of our climbing route. We started the climb on fixed rope and then moved to free climbing – at a difficulty level between 5.6 and 5.8 – and reached the top ridge by 9:00 AM. I carried in my pocket a copy of Heinreich Harrer's route description from his book and referred to it often. Ripto, one of our Indonesian guides, explained that we were blessed to be above a huge cloud /fog bank obscuring everything below us because, he said, we couldn't see that we were very high and very exposed – and fortunate that we couldn't actually see just how exposed we actually were. After many time consuming belays, rappels, and fixed line traverses along the ridge, we all reached the summit by 1:45 PM. Todd was especially excited since this was his seventh continental highpoint! Our celebration was cut short since it was storming – of course – with snow, hail, thunder and lightning. And since we were the highest point around for thousands of miles, we beat a hasty retreat.

Our descent down the mountain was a series of long rappels, 150 – 300 ft. at a time, but still took us until dark to reach the bottom since only one person can rappel on a rope at a time. And when the last person was finishing the final rappel, by headlamp, a rock came loose and struck him on his head and shoulder - bouncing off and hitting a second person on the wrist who was waiting at the bottom. We put off fully assessing the extent of those injuries and high-tailed it back to camp, in heavy rain (of course), by headlamp – reaching it by 8:00 PM for a fifteen hour day. After a quick snack, we all went straight to bed. We were done in!

The next day, a declared and well-earned rest day, Todd took off, with Ogun, to the Freeport Mine to inquire about medical support for our shoulder and wrist injuries – and to inquire about making our exit through the mine property to save another 5 – 6 day slog back through the jungle to Ilaga. He did succeed in getting the mine management to agree to have one of their doctors examine our injured, but denied our request to egress through the mine. The next day, as we escorted our injured to the mine property for their shuttle to their exams, Todd drafted a second, more pleading appeal for their support to short circuit our departure.

The first good news is that x-rays confirmed that our climber's injuries were only sprains – nothing broken. And the second was that the mine personnel would give all of us – not including the Dani natives – an escort to their mining village of Tembagapura – where we spent the night in jail, under constant police observation, until the morning mining bus arrived at 4 AM to take us to Timika – a town on the southern coast of West New Guinea.

Now, the good news was that we escaped a five to six day slog back through mud and rain to Ilaga and, instead flew directly back to Biak from Timika, while the bad news was that our passports, of course, were still in Ilaga!

Henry Todd and Ripto flew back to New Guinea the next day to attempt to retrieve all of our passports, but they were only able to gather up their own. This initiated a variety of urgent phone calls to Jakarta, the capitol of Indonesia, to attempt to resolve this. A day later, and another expensive round trip charter flight to New Guinea, got us our passports and we were soon on our way to Honolulu and Los Angeles that night.

One more continental highpoint successfully climbed.

Mt. Vinson (Antarctica)

In January 2014 I had a very special opportunity to extend my list of continental highpoints climbed to six with a trip to Antarctic's highpoint, Mt. Vinson, at 16,160 ft. with my son Scott. What a special treat that was.

While Mt. Vinson is not especially technically demanding, it is guaranteed to be chilly around there, even in the Antarctica summer, and especially so on its summit. And the logistics of getting there and back are --- challenging.

There are today a large number of scientific research stations spread all over the Antarctic continent, and they all need to be regularly re-supplied with food, fuel, personnel, and equipment – at least throughout the Antarctic's summer season. Managing all of those logistics requirements is an American outfit, Antarctic Logistics and Expeditions (ALE) based in Punta Arenas, Chile. They fly a huge Russian Ilyushin 76 cargo plane, chartered from Almaty Air Cargo Service, Kazakhstan, to shuttle people and supplies to a logistics base called Union Glacier, with its 2 mile long ice runway, on the Antarctic continent, every two weeks or so. These flights are usually spoken for many months in advance, and getting a seat on such a flight puts one in direct competition with important scientists who are doing research there, but it is possible.

We made the required arrangements with the help of Alpine Ascents International (AAI), who I had climbed with a number of times previously, and were delighted to discover that one of our two guides would be Vern Tejas who I had climbed with on Mt. McKinley 27 years earlier. We were delighted to discover that Vern was still climbing these many years later.

Scott and I not only had to pass muster with AAI, but we also had to meet stringent medical requirements set by ALE since they didn't want to fly someone onto the Antarctic continent who could become a health liability for them.

Shortly after arriving in Punta Arenas, Chile, via Santiago, we attended a detailed briefing by ALE as to the requirements regarding waste management, etc., once on the cold continent. Then we went through an extensive equipment review before departure since there aren't a lot of outdoor stores available in Antarctica.

Our crew consisted of two guides, Vern and Garrett Madison, and eight clients. Vern and Garrett decided to break us into two rope teams, with each of them guiding a team of four clients. Garrett was to guide his group of four clients consisting of a young brother/sister pair from Pakistan, a 68 year old Dutchman, and a 69 year old retired army officer from Australia – while Vern had Scott and me and a husband/ wife team, Ankur and Sangeeta, from India. Our two groups certainly had an international flavor. Ankur had spent all of his adult life at sea as a merchant cargo ship captain. Sangeeta was very pleasant, but seemed lost without her personal servant to assist her with everything. She told us that she took her servant with her on her training hikes to carry her pack when she got tired.

The very next day, after our briefing, ALE got clearance to fly and we were soon off for our 4 ½ hour flight to the Union Glacier camp. Being basically a military plane, its windows were tiny and didn't provide much of a view while airborne, but there was a camera aimed out the pilot's front window and transmitted to a huge TV screen at the front of the cargo area where we were, so we had excellent views of our take-off and landing. The rest of the time the views were basically ---- lots and lots of white snow and ice! Upon landing we were met by Vern who had already made arrangements for a flight the following day, by Twin Otter equipped with skis, to our Base Camp on the Branscomb Glacier, about 120 miles away, at the base of Mt. Vinson. Mt Vinson is at the very southern end of the Ellsworth Mountain Range. This was going to be Vern's 35th ascent of Mt. Vinson. So, once more, we were in good, experienced hands.

It was cold and windy, but very clear. And with the sun out 24 hours a day, we had lots of schedule flexibility following that flight.

After taking a full day at Base Camp to get organized and packed for our climb – as well as rehearsing some techniques for climbing while roped, crevasse self-rescue, and other similar tasks - we were off to our first of two camps on the mountain. This lower camp, at about 9,000 ft. elevation, was about 2,000 ft. above our base camp – over generally easy terrain. Since our climb was near the end of the climbing season there, our route was generally well defined – which reduced the risk of falling into a crevasse. We were all roped to one another anyway. Each of us was carrying a full pack and pulling a loaded plastic sled so that we could establish our Low Camp with only one trip. We were there in about 7 hours.

Even though the sun was shining 24 hours a day in the Antarctic summer, temperatures inside the tent were around zero degrees when we were in the shade of a nearby mountain, but went up to almost 50° F when we were in the direct sun. Vern prepared and served all of our meals inside the kitchen tent which had benches cut into the snow pack for us to sit on while we awaited our meals. This tent also served as his sleeping tent. One fun feature each evening, following dinner, was when Vern would call stateside on his satellite phone to a special website maintained by AAI which would record his message and make it available to anyone logging in to this special website. That way we could keep folks back home up to date on our progress.

That next day we carried a load to the bottom of a very long and steep slope. Our plan was to shuttle this load up this slope the next day, but high winds kept us pinned down in camp that day. We did manage to haul our loads up the slope the following day – getting them almost to our High Camp location before returning to Low Camp.

Following that we lost yet another day to high winds, but then were able to break camp and reach our High Camp at 12,400 ft. elevation a day later by 8:00 PM – including our loads stashed two days earlier. We set up our tents, secured them from the winds, had dinner, and were in our sleeping bags by 11:30 PM. This was certainly our hardest day so far – especially for Sangeeta – but we all made it.

We were originally planning to have a rest day here, but with more high winds due in soon, we were up at 7:00 AM that next morning and left for the summit by 8:00 AM. And with only occasional rest stops for snacks and drink, we were on the summit by 4:00 PM. We took all of the usual summit photos, under very cold and windy conditions – with temps around -10° F to -20° F – and then high-tailed it back to High Camp – reaching it by 8:00 PM that evening. We were elated. One more summit success!

(Garrett had gotten his group of four to the summit a day earlier.)

The following morning we broke camp, descended the steep slope, recovered our plastic sleds at Low Camp, and made it back to our Base Camp by the middle of the afternoon – where, by radio, we requested a Twin Otter pick-up as soon as practical. We were expecting it that next morning.

While we were finishing up dinner that evening, Vern asked each of us what else we might want. Ankur and Sangeeta only wanted a quick return to civilization where they could get a hot shower. When he turned to me, I, half-jokingly, said that I'd really like a cold beer! He stared at me for a minute and then disappeared from the tent – returning ten minutes later – with a 6-pack of beer! Naturally it was cold – everything in Antarctica is cold! To this day I have no idea where he got the beer, but it certainly hit the spot. Scott and I were in hog heaven now! The beer came with a caution to store any unused bottles in our sleeping bags lest they freeze solid.

The next morning the Twin Otter was in to fly us back to Union Glacier – and the very next day the Ilyushin 76 cargo plane was in from Chile. Vern got us manifested onto its return flight and we were quickly back in Chile – none the worse for wear. And, following a wonderful restaurant meal in Punta Arenas with our whole team that evening, Scott and I were soon on our flight back home.

Our sixth continental highpoint was now in the books.

Chapter Three

State Highpoints

California: 1967: When I was stationed at Fort Huachuca, Arizona, in the army in 1967, I was offered a unique adventure opportunity that I just couldn't turn down. Early in my time as a test officer at the army's Electronic Proving Ground I befriended Herb Ide, a civilian liaison officer there. He knew that I enjoyed the outdoors and so he invited me to join him and some friends on a two day hike over the upcoming Labor Day weekend to the top of Mt. Whitney in California. Mt. Whitney, at 14,494 ft., was not only the highest mountain in California, but it was also the highest mountain in the contiguous 48 states – located near the southern end of California's famous Sierra Nevada mountain range. Since this was almost 10,000 ft. higher than I had ever been before, I was immediately interested. Of course, it also intimidated me at the same time. But when Herb, a 55 year old, who also suffered from seriously diminished capacity in both lungs, told me that he had climbed it several times previously, I decided to give it a try. I trained in earnest every chance I could get between then and our departure date, and, at 26, was undoubtedly in the best shape of my life. Surely I could make this peak in good form.

We drove to California – Herb, three of his close friends, and me - that September, stopping at the Inyo National Forest Headquarters in Lone Pine, California, long enough to pick up our permit and then headed to a B&B in the Alabama Hills, the foothills to the famous Sierras, for a night's sleep.

Right at sun-up, we drove up to Whitney Portal, the trailhead at the end of the road, and loaded up our backpacks for this 22 mile roundtrip overnight walk in the wild. I didn't know any of the other of my hiking companions, but we soon got into a rhythm together and by late afternoon arrived at Mirror Lake, at about 12,000 ft. elevation - our campsite for the night – right beneath the Sierra Crest and Mt. Whitney itself. I was jazzed and had a hard time sleeping that night since I was so excited.

At first light we were up and ready to hike to the summit. I quickly out-distanced the other hikers, but not Herb. He was easily holding his own – the whole way to the summit ridge and along that ridge toward the final summit slope. And just when I was hoping for a short rest break – with the summit less than 45 minutes away – and well ahead of the rest of our group - Herb said, "If you don't mind, I'll just go on to the summit at my own pace and meet you on top. The final route is very obvious from here." I was flabbergasted! I decided that no 55 year old – with faulty lungs – was going to beat me up this final slope when I was, at 26, my fittest ever. But he did! He congratulated me when I finally got there – huffing and puffing! The others arrived another 45 minutes to a full hour later. Herb really handed me my hat on that climb! And I've never forgotten it. But I was very excited to have extended my highest climbing altitude by almost 10,000 ft. with no ill side effects. I couldn't wait for more.

But my fun wasn't over. Herb "commissioned" one of our tech writers back at the post to draft up a story of our little hike and got it published in the post newspaper that next week – along with a photo of the two of us on top of Mt. Whitney. From that write-up you would think that we had just scaled Mt. Everest itself. I got a lot of free publicity out of that article.

1982: As it would happen, shortly after moving to Arizona from New York, I returned to Mt. Whitney two more times. The first of those two return trips, in 1982, was with an old friend, Richard Kast, from IBM in New York, who had transferred to San Jose, California, around the same time that I moved to Arizona. We had worked up a week-long backpacking plan to hike up Mt. Whitney from its west side – via the popular John Muir Trail - and along the way climb three other 14,000 ft. peaks: Williamson, Tyndall, and Muir. Richard's friend, Tim Halpern, joined us, too. Our plan called for us to reach the west side of the Sierras from the town of Independence, just north of Lone Pine. We would hike ten miles up and over Shepherd Pass – camping for the night right at the base of Mt. Williamson and Mt. Tyndall.

In the morning I headed up the route to the summit of Williamson, a Class 3 climb, and, for some reason, got well ahead of Richard and Tim. Since I had pointed out the route to them the previous evening, I was sure that they could follow me, but, for some reason, they got off route, couldn't safely proceed, and went back to our camp. I missed having them join me on the summit – my second ever 14,000 ft. peak.

We then tackled Mt. Tyndall, staying together this time, and made the summit – in good order. But on the way back down Richard spied a narrow snow slope that went clear to the bottom and decided that sliding down it would be far quicker than walking down. And so, with a long stick under his arm to act as a brake, he sat down in the snow and launched himself. Everything went well enough until his braking stick broke – and then he had no effective way of slowing his descent. He started hollering loudly, as he sped up, suggesting to me that he had been injured, but when I finally got down to him to check him out, I discovered that he had ripped the bottom of his jeans from stem to stern exposing his underside and accumulating snow up his back until it was coming out of his shirt up near his ears! Needless to say, he was up late that night in his sleeping bag sewing up his britches by flashlight.

On this trip I was experimenting with another interesting scheme. The idea of lightweight backpacking had really taken off full force and every backpacker was continually looking for ways to cut every single ounce of weight from his pack. I had already traded up a lot of my backpacking gear for lighter stuff, but continued to look for even more weight reduction. And I found it – I thought. I had stumbled across a recipe for a modern day version of pemmican – the high energy dried food used by native Indians when they were on the move. My pemmican recipe included a variety of high energy ingredients that were mixed up and pressed out on a cookie sheet, like brownies, and then baked lightly. This is then cut up into squares, packaged in zip-lock bags – weighed out for breakfasts, lunches, and dinners – according to my special nutrition formula. Backpacking with this food obviated the need for stoves, fuel, pots, bowls, and utensils – saving tons of weight. This was going to be the ultimate in lightweight backpacking. It would revolutionize the whole strategy of lightweight backpacking – I thought.

Kay, my wife, while more than a bit skeptical, agreed to assemble and mix the ingredients, bake it, and help me package it up in single meal zip-lock bags. My pack was now so light that it almost hiked by itself! I was stoked. (Needless to say, Richard and Tim were – skeptical – to say the least.)

I had packed for our week together: seven breakfasts, seven lunches, and seven dinners – all designed to give me the required nourishment for a week of strenuous backpacking at high elevations.

As it turned out, it was good for our first on-the-trail lunch and dinner. By the next morning's breakfast I wasn't looking forward to this "pemmican" with the same enthusiasm, but I just stuck the bag in my pocket and headed off down the trail. Sure enough, by mid-morning I was ready for some food and those bars worked – barely. And it went downhill from there. It turns out that the one thing I hadn't factored in to this plan was taste! In fact, this "pemmican" tasted – just awful! Soon it was everything I could do to choke it down – and that only after starving myself for hours. And, when I got within a couple days of the end of our week together, I stopped eating it completely. I just couldn't stomach it at all. It was simply terrible! What a miscalculation! When we finally got back to the trailhead, after a full week of backpacking and mountain climbing, I was ready to eat the north side of a south bound cow!

And when I finally got back home and reported my experience to Kay, she said simply, "I could have told you so!" So much for that experiment. Lesson learned. But I had managed to successfully scale our four 14'rs – including a successful second ascent for me of Mt. Whitney. That made it worthwhile.

1984: I repeated this backpacking week in the Sierras two years later with Scott, at 14, and it came off without a hitch – including all four mountain peaks. Well, almost without a hitch. Our very first freeze-dried dinner turned out to be totally inedible for some reason. (I wonder if that had anything to do with the fact that I had gotten them for free.) We simply dumped it and cooked up the next night's dinner instead – which worked until the end of the week when we found ourselves, of course, one dinner short. Oh well, at that point we still had one breakfast left, so we ate that instead and accepted the fact that we would be hiking out in the morning on an empty stomach.

Scott was especially proud of the fact that our pack weight for the entire week was well under 30 pounds apiece at the start and, of course, went down further every day as we ate our meals for that day. In fact, Scott really bragged it up when we came on some other backpackers with pack weights up around 60 lbs. apiece. They were especially delighted when Scott relieved them of some of their weight - and we ate our fill of pounds and pounds of M & M's for the rest of our trip!

The idea of climbing other state highpoints never held any special appeal to me – though when I lived in New York my friends and I did manage to summit the highpoints of New York, Vermont, New Hampshire, and Maine.

This all changed when, in 1999, my international climbing friend, Steve Bridges, told me that he was well on his way to having been to the highest point in every one of the 50 states. He only had four more to go to complete his list and wanted my help with three of them: the highpoints of Oregon, Wyoming, and Montana. These three all involved a summit covered with ice and snow – no place to be found alone. And so I agreed to help him here. Besides, it seemed like a good adventure.

Oregon: The state's highpoint, Mt. Hood, at 11,239 ft., is located 47 miles due east of Portland. Steve Bridges had made an earlier attempt on Mt. Hood on a guided climb, but got stopped short by a storm. While not making the summit then, he now had an excellent idea of the proper route to use. He was satisfied that, given good weather, he and I could successfully manage our way to the summit. And so, in June 1999, since I already had plans to be in northern California on a climb with Scott, I offered to drive further north after that trip and meet Steve at the Portland Airport. We would, together, make our own attempt on Mt. Hood.

I picked him up right on schedule and we drove east to a small town called Government Camp and arranged for a room for the night. We then drove the additional 5 miles up the road to Timberline Lodge, at 6,000 ft., right at the start of the south side route, the most popular route up Mt. Hood.

The route to the summit from this lodge is only 4 ½ miles, but with an elevation gain of about 5,300 ft. Since the weather appeared stable, our intention was to start our hike at midnight that very night. We would climb with headlamps under the ski lift, using the ski lift pylons as our guideposts, and then, upon reaching the top of the lift line, angle east and continue climbing up to an obvious ridge, called the Hogsback. This ridge would lead us directly to the final snow slope. There is a major crevasse, called a bergschrund, between the east end of the Hogsback ridge and the final slope, but from our position in the lodge's parking lot, it looked to be bridged by snow and passable. The only remaining question then was how to safely ascend the final snow slope. That's when it occurred to us that we might need some snow pickets to use as snow anchors as we relayed one another with a rope up this final slope. (A snow picket is a two foot long piece of rigid angle aluminum – pointed on one end and with a nylon loop tied on the other end.) And, of course, coming from Arizona, we were a little short on snow pickets in our kit bag!

But we did see a couple climbers coming down the ski slope toward us. When they arrived at the parking lot I asked them if they had successfully summited and inquired as to whether they needed snow pickets on that final slope. The one climber immediately looked at me and responded, "I wouldn't climb that slope without snow pickets!"

I looked at Steve, he looked at me, and we immediately ran to the truck and drove quickly back to Portland where we knew there to be an REI store - hoping that they carried snow pickets. We got there in quick time and the good news was that they had snow pickets – displayed right in their front window. The bad news was that just as we arrived, the owner was locking up for the night and wouldn't be open again until 8:30 in the morning. We managed to locate another outdoor store, but it, too, was closed for the night. Bummer! A night wasted! We returned to Government Camp and drowned our disappointment in cold beer and hot pizza. We did get a good night's sleep and returned to Portland in the morning for a couple snow pickets. We also realized that if the snow on that final slope was especially consolidated or frozen, we'd need some sort of hammer to place our new pickets firmly. Of course, we didn't have any sort of piton hammer with us – or even an ice axe with a hammerhead end on it. So we stopped at an Ace Hardware store and bought a conventional carpenter's hammer, had the clerk drill a hole in its handle for an attachment cord, and we were ready for the mountain.

That night, at midnight, we signed the hiker's register at the Timberline Lodge and headed up the mountain – with the weather still holding. Hours later, just as the sun was starting to think about rising, we arrived at the east end of the Hogsback ridge for our first close-up view of the crevasse between us and that final snow slope. Yes, it was a very impressive crevasse, easily big enough to swallow a house whole! But there was a snow bridge across it leading directly to our final snow slope – with hundreds of footprints on it. We were in luck.

But the longer I looked at this steep snow slope, the more that I was comfortable that, with care, I could safely negotiate this slope with crampons and ice axe alone. I broached the subject cautiously with Steve and he agreed. So, after all of our trouble, we ditched our day packs, harnesses, rope, and, yes, the snow pickets, too, and ventured cautiously across the crevasse's snow bridge and proceeded up the snow slope – with all due care and caution. In very short order we were above the steep section and proceeded on to the summit just as the sun rose in full splendor.

Heading back down the same slope – only minutes later – with, once more, all due caution and soon were reunited with our packs, rope, and brand new, unused snow pickets. Now there was nothing left for us to do except trudge back downhill to the parking lot – elated that we had one more state highpoint under our belt.

Upon arriving back at the parking lot, we were approached by two fellows who had been studying the route themselves. One of them asked me whether we needed snow pickets on the final snow slope. I smiled, winked at Steve, and told the fellow, "I wouldn't climb that slope without snow pickets!"

Wyoming: Two months later, in August 1999, we started for Gannett Peak which, at 13,804 ft. elevation, and right on the Continental Divide, was the highest point in Wyoming – just 38 ft. higher than Wyoming's famous Grand Teton. Gannett is located 23 trail miles inside Bridger National Forest, in the Wind River Range, so we used parts of two days to get in the 17 miles to Upper Titcomb Lake at about 10,600 ft. elevation – just one short ridge from the base of the final climb. This is also where the snow level began. And that's where we made our camp – planning to make our summit effort early the next morning with day packs.

Steve had invited on our trip one of his co-workers, Neil Barrett (who has since shared many other outdoor adventures with me). Steve even loaned Neil an extra set of crampons and an ice axe that he had, but hadn't given him any instructions on how to use them. So, shortly after arriving at the lake and setting up our tents, I gave Neil a crash course in crampon and ice axe use.

At first light we hiked to the base of the final summit climb before donning our crampons, and then one final uphill slog put us on the summit – without incident – in great, sunny, blue sky weather.

By the time that we descended, we discovered that the snow surface had softened up from the warm sun and so snow began balling up on the bottoms of our crampons. This caused each of us more than once to lose our footing, fall, and start sliding down slope - stopping only when we used our ice axes to stop our slide. At this point Neil was thankful for his earlier mini-class in ice axe use. A little over a day later we were back out to the trailhead and on our way to Montana.

Montana: OK, now this highpoint, Granite Peak, should be quick and easy. It's 10 miles north of the state line, inside Custer National Forest, at an elevation of only 12,799 ft. and the directions to it are straightforward. From the town of Fishtail, Montana, drive west to the hydroelectric plant at the head of Mystic lake, hike west to the other end of the lake and turn south at Huckleberry Creek. Hike up the trail in that drainage to Avalanche Lake at 9,870 ft. and the peak should be right in front of us. But then maybe there's a reason that this was the last state highpoint to be climbed; even Alaska's Mt. McKinley was summited ten years before someone successfully climbed Granite Peak.

Our hike in and up to Avalanche Lake, about 8 ½ miles, did go pretty much according to this outline, but it also managed to consume the entire day what with all of the blow down, rock hoping, and a rainstorm to deal with. We camped for the night on the east side of Avalanche Lake planning to start our ascent at first light. But we couldn't turn in without first surrounding our tents with mousetraps and moth balls! We had been warned to bring such amenities to deal with the mouse scourge there. And, sure enough, even before falling asleep, our traps were going off left and right!

At first light we were up and on our way for the final two miles to the summit. Our first obstacle was an extensive field of gigantic boulders – from car size up to house size – interlaced with cobwebs and hairy black spiders! Once through that obstacle we looked straight up at a steep, continuous 1,000 ft. snow slope. This was manageable with our crampons and ice axes, but it left no room for error, because a slip would have meant a long, fast slide into the rock field at the bottom.

Once having that slope safely scaled, plus one smaller additional snow field, we could stash our crampons and ice axes and revert to steep rock climbing and route finding for the next couple hours. Our climbing rope got good use here.

In due time, to our delight, we managed to finally summit this massive rock pile in continuously stable weather.

We sped up our descent through this upper rocky section with a series of rope rappels and were quickly back to our steep snow slope. Time, once again, for serious concentration during this descent. Another hour saw us through the ugly, spider-filled boulder field, and we were back in camp – after a 10 – 11 hour day – fully done in. We busied ourselves resetting mousetraps while we waited for water to boil for our dinner preparation

– wishing for some cold beers with which to celebrate our success. Some climbers consider this ascent to be the toughest technical challenge of the 50 state high points. We were not inclined to disagree at this point.

Postscript: This climb of Granite Peak gave Steve 49 of the 50 state highpoints to his credit; he only needed Hawaii's 13,796 ft. Mauna Kea to complete his 50 state list. I gladly offered to fly to Hawaii with him to gain this final peak, but, for some reason that I'll never understand, he elected to take his bride with him instead and made a relaxing week of it.

Nevada: Despite our success with climbing the highpoints of Oregon, Wyoming, and Montana, I still had no particular interest in reaching all of the other state highpoints. However, I started to get interested in hiking the highpoints of the western states since these represented a little more of a challenge than "hiking" to the highpoint of, say, Florida's Britton Hill at 345 ft. or Delaware's Tower Hill at 451 ft. above sea level.

So, on my way home from California in June 1999, I intentionally chose a route that would allow me to tackle the highpoint of Nevada – Boundary Peak – at 13,140 ft. Boundary Peak is at the very northern end of the White Mountain Range (the rest of which is in California) right on the Nevada – California border. I was able to round up a detailed description of how to get to the trailhead – an involved assortment of state and county roads and 16 miles of bumpy dirt/sand roads. My initial plan was to spend the night at the trailhead and hike the peak early the next morning. I didn't really have any meals with me, but figured on getting by with a handful of energy bars. Having nothing better to do, I took a late afternoon walk down the trail toward Boundary Peak to check things out. The trail distance to the summit was only supposed to be a little over two miles!

A short ways down the trail I couldn't help but notice that there was a substantial mountain coming into view to my left front. And since my map said to look for Boundary Peak in that direction, I, of course, assumed that I was looking at Boundary Peak itself! I weighed my options for a brief couple moments and quickly jogged back to the truck for my hiking boots. Yes, it was quite late in the afternoon by then, but I just figured that I could squeeze in this climb and be back in time to reach a real restaurant and motel for the night.

In short order I was on my way back down the trail – with day pack, water, a wind breaker, an energy bar – and a head lamp. I was soon back to my previous spot and continued down the trail at just short of a jog – only to discover that developing right next to my candidate target peak was an even taller peak – which must surely now be the real Boundary Peak! Oops! Darn! Time for re-evaluation. It was now after 4:00 in the afternoon with the sun racing for the horizon. In a split second I decided to go for it – now almost at full jog - watching for some evidence where the trail would start veering uphill toward this new summit. (I later on came to understand that my first target peak was named, appropriately enough, False Peak, at only 900 ft. lower than Boundary Peak itself.) I did manage to spy a semblance of an uphill route in front of me that looked to be almost a real trail and took it – climbing as fast as possible. I reached the summit at 7:15 PM and hunted around for some sort of marker or register denoting this to actually be Boundary Peak and didn't relax until I found it. Now, with the sun fully set, I took careful note of my descent route, donned my windbreaker over a wringing wet shirt, quickly ate my one energy bar, and high-tailed it back down the mountain – not resting until I was back on the established trail. From here on I could relax and focus on not losing the trail as it got even darker. I reached the truck right at 9:00 PM – and could now relax – having gotten off-trail and lost only once along the way. Now to drive back out of there and find a restaurant for a well-earned meal – with one more state highpoint checked off.

Washington: Mt. Rainier, Washington State's highpoint, just 40 miles southeast of Tacoma, is in a class by itself. First, at 14,411 ft. elevation, it is the second highest mountain in the lower 48 states after California's Mt. Whitney. Second, due to its near coastal location, it is subject to severe storms 12 months of the year and, as a result, is continually covered with deep snow and ice – resulting in numerous ice walls, unstable snow, and dangerous crevasses. And, third, it is inside the Rainier National Park and the park management has established skill requirements for anyone attempting to climb this peak.

Most people choose to satisfy this requirement by signing up with one of several park-certified mountain guide services to lead them to the summit. And I was no exception.

In August 2005 I signed on with Rainier Mountaineering, a guide service run by Lou Whittaker, twin brother to Jim Whittaker, the first American to summit Mt. Everest. On Day 1 I attended a class in the snow up on the mountain where we practiced walking with crampons, hiking roped up in teams, and rehearsed how to execute self-arrest with an ice axe while sliding down a snowy slope. On Day 2 we hiked up to Camp Muir at the 10,000 ft. level on Mt. Rainier where we fixed dinner and turned in right at sunset – only to be awakened at midnight for a quick breakfast and packing up for a night-time assault on the mountain. Leaving Camp Muir by headlamp, under the leadership of Peter Whittaker, Lou's son, at 1:00 AM, while the snow was stable and still frozen, and rock fall was less, we headed up the mountain. We reached the summit crater at 6:30 AM – right at sun-up. Some of us continued across the crater floor to the opposite side of the crater where the highest point on the rim was located and, after the celebratory photos, were back at Camp Muir by late morning and at the bottom by early afternoon. One more state highpoint completed.

Idaho: Returning home from my 2005 climb of Mt. Rainier in Washington, I chose a route home that took me through southern Idaho – watching for the tiny town of Mackay because twenty miles north of Mackay, right off US 93, is the trailhead for 12,662 ft. Borah Peak, Idaho state's highpoint. I checked out its exact location for the trailhead before turning in for the night. It was easy to find and there was ample parking right at the trailhead.

I was up well before dawn for what should have been a very straightforward climb only to discover that I had inadvertently selected the one day of the year when all of the locals join together to climb the mountain in commemoration of something or another. There were dozens and dozens of cars already parked on the road at the trailhead and more arriving every minute! So I was certainly warmed up by the time that I walked from my parking spot well down the road to the trailhead.

The hike, while consistently very steep, covering well over 5,000 ft. of elevation in 3 ¼ miles, was very straightforward, except for having to safely pass hundreds of other hikers on a twisting, rocky trail. But summit I did in something under three hours. Another two hours and I was back at the bottom and on my way home. In the category of "you can't believe everything that you read," one guidebook reference that I used for this hike recommended that I plan on 12 – 14 hours to round-trip it! So much for that recommendation.

Utah: Once more, almost on the spur of the moment, while I was returning home from another bike tour in Washington State in early August 2006, I chose a route down through Utah. Stopping for gas in Ogden, Utah, I reviewed my map and trail information to Utah's highpoint, Kings Peak. This highpoint is at 13,528 ft. elevation in the High Uintas Primitive Area inside Wasatch National Forest, just south of the Wyoming border, and it wasn't all that far east of where I was. So, quick like a bunny, I drove over to the Kings Peak Trailhead at the Henry Fork Campground, put on my hiking boots, grabbed my pack, and headed off down the trail. I was pretty lightly loaded: only a light weight sleeping bag, a sleeping pad, a waterproof bivy sack to cover the sleeping bag, a jacket, headlamp, water, and a handful of energy bars. My "plan" was to get as far down the 12 mile trail as I could by nightfall, and then complete the hike to the summit that next morning – and return.

But, once more, I was stoked, and by late afternoon I was at timberline, within a short walk of Gunsight Pass – which was supposed to be only 1 ½ miles from the Kings Peak summit. And, more importantly, to its immediate west was a substantial peak – that I figured just had to be Kings Peak. This one would be easy – I thought. But to be sure, I took a bearing on this peak with my compass and consulted my map. Yep, that was exactly the correct bearing from my position for Kings Peak. And it was easily reachable before sundown. None the less, I carefully marked my position on the trail with some rocks, stepped off the trail exactly ten steps to stash my pack in the brush, and headed up the trail - watching for a side trail up to the peak.

Right in the pass there was a semblance of a trail leading up to the top, and so I took it already planning my hike back to the truck. In short order I arrived at the top, but failed to find any sort of marker or register marking this as Utah's highpoint. And then I lifted my head and discovered an even higher mountain in the distance – with an obvious trail heading up to its summit! Oops! Once more, in my exuberance I had climbed the wrong mountain! And the sun was racing toward the horizon. Darn! Shades of Boundary Peak! As Yogi Berra would have said, "This feels like deja vu all over again." But, heck, I'm committed now, so off I went downhill, trying not to stumble on the loose rock, reached the summit trail, and headed up the correct peak wondering where I had gone wrong. It was still light when I summited, but not by much, so I memorized the route back to the main trail to Gunsight Pass and took off back down – getting in as much distance as possible while I could still see the trail. It was pitch black by the time that I reached the main trail, but now I was confident that I'd be OK. I walked up through Gunsight Pass and back down the trail on the opposite side for almost 45 minutes before spying my marker rocks. I turned 90 degrees and stepped off exactly ten steps and looked around. No pack! Oops! What went wrong? Back out to the trail, locate the marker rocks and try this again. But still no pack! I even tried hiking further down the tail to see if, by chance, there was, for some reason, another set of marker rocks – to no avail. Back to my rocks. Let's try this again – but this time with ten <u>big</u> steps. And, lo and behold, there was my pack! Hurray for me! I'm going to survive this one after all. Within ten minutes I had everything unrolled and set up, removed my sweaty clothes, and crawled inside where I was quickly toasty warm. One energy bar later and I was sound asleep!

The hike back to the truck in the early morning was very pleasant since I had this highpoint behind me. Yes, it's an easy enough hike – if you do it all in daylight. The real challenge is hiking it by the dark of the moon!

Colorado: I have spent any number of weeks in Colorado scaling a great many of Colorado's 58 peaks over 14,000 ft. elevation. But I've almost always been with son Scott or a friend who have already climbed Colorado's highpoint, Mt. Elbert, at 14,443 ft. and so I had not been able to push to include that peak in our weekly climbing plan. My opportunity came in August 2012, when, after a week of climbing 14'rs there, I found myself alone with nothing better to do, and so, departing after a rainy night in Leadville, I was on the trail, by myself, up Mt. Elbert at first light. The top was still totally socked in with clouds, but the route was fairly easy to follow: keep going up until you run out of up! Near the top ridge I entered the cloud bank where visibility dropped to about twenty feet, walking in six inches of fresh snow, and snow flurries in the air. The monument marking the top was fairly easy to locate because there was a wedding ceremony just finishing up beside it as I arrived. I had been hiking for 2 hours 40 minutes, so I hadn't wasted any time in that ascent. Dressed only in shorts and a T-shirt, I didn't plan on hanging around the top very long, but I was told that had I arrived ten minutes earlier, I could have stood in for the best man who was, I guess, a no-show for the ceremony. Shucks, I might have gotten to kiss the bride! One more western state highpoint checked off the list.

New Mexico: The highpoint of New Mexico is Wheeler Peak which, at 13,161 ft., is located at the Taos Ski Valley ski center, 31 miles north of the city of Taos. A hike from near the ski center, on a marked trail, in the Wheeler Peak Wilderness, a part of the greater Carson National Forest, goes through a beautiful forest to a marked summit with impressive views in every direction. The hike is a little over 7 miles long and just under 4,000 ft. of elevation gain. I hiked it early one morning following a week of hiking 14'rs in Colorado in July 2012, and returned in time to enjoy lunch with an old friend, who owned Eske's Brew Pub in downtown Taos, before continuing my drive home.

Arizona: Humphreys Peak, at 12,633 ft. elevation, Arizona's highest point, is the highest of three prominent volcanic summits in the San Francisco Mountains just north of Flagstaff. With an elevation gain of 3,500 ft. from the parking lot at the Arizona Snow Bowl Ski Center to its summit, almost 5 miles one way, it's pretty much an all-day effort to round-trip it if you include sightseeing north to the Grand Canyon, east to the Painted Desert, south to Flagstaff and the White Mountains, and west to the Colorado Plateau. I've hiked it in the early fall when the colors are changing, in the winter in snowshoes, and in the late spring with clear trails in the open and three feet of snow in the forest. It is always a memorable experience.

Texas: On the occasion of escorting some friends to see the famous Carlsbad Caverns in southern New Mexico back in 1998, we stopped off in Guadalupe Mountains National Park, just east of El Paso, Texas, and hiked to the summit of Guadalupe Peak at 8,749 ft. This hike of about 4 ½ miles and an elevation gain of just under 3,000 ft. would have been unremarkable except that, as a result of a recently ended rain storm, the mountain trail was completely consumed by a heavy fog bank – with visibility reduced to only 10–15 feet. This continued until we had gained about 2,000 ft. at which point we broke out of these clouds to a spectacularly brilliant, sunshiny day – with visibility for miles and miles – of more cloud banks. (It had all dissipated in time for our return trip so that we could see on the way down what we had missed on the way up.)

In true Texas fashion we fully expected to see on top a massive Texas-style sign announcing this to be Texas's highpoint, but, in fact, we almost missed the small announcement plaque mounted near the ground on the summit rock. There was, though, to our surprise, a massive memorial sign on top placed there by American Airlines commemorating all of their pilots who had lost their lives over the years while flying for American.

Chapter Four

Mountaineering

Ama Dablam / Grand Teton: When our planned 1992 trip to Carstensz Pyramid fell through, following Indonesia's withdrawal of our climbing permit, our expeditioner, InnerAsia Expeditions, offered to transfer our down payment to a climbing expedition being run by their partner, Alpine Ascents International (AAI). AAI was planning a climb of a mountain called Ama Dablam at 22,349 ft. elevation. I had to admit, frankly, that I had not ever heard of it before. But when I learned that it was a very classic mountain, in Nepal, right off the trail to Mt. Everest, I immediately got interested. My good friend Steve Bridges was also interested. So we signed up.

Ama Dablam, which means "mother's locket" in Nepalese, was named after a large snow block hanging in the middle of a large snow field on its upper western face. It was first summited by Barry Bishop in 1961 on an expedition put together by Sir Edmund Hillary, who was the first to summit Mt. Everest.

Ama Dablam is considered to be one of the four peaks in the world that have a classic stand-alone pyramidal shape – the others being the Matterhorn in Switzerland, Alpamayo in the Cordillera Blanca range of central Peru, and Assiniboine in British Columbia.

So we were excited to be considered for such a classic climb – especially since it was located within walking distance of the well-known Mt. Everest.

Once our down payment was accepted, we were told that in order to participate in this expedition, we'd have to first get approved by Pete Athans, one of our two mountain guides. (The other guide was Todd Burleson, owner and chief guide of AAI.) That was unexpected, but I made a point of contacting him. (He was spending that summer as a climbing guide in the Grand Teton National Park in Jackson, Wyoming.) He "suggested" that we come up to Jackson and climb the Grand Teton – with him. And after he brought it up three different times in our conversation, I started taking him seriously. That was intimidating for sure, but we agreed to do it because we really wanted to have a shot at climbing Ama Dablam – and having nothing better to do (except possibly perish on that treacherous mountain!) we signed up.

But we sure didn't want to fail our test, so we went up to Jackson early in order to take a couple of refresher courses in rock climbing before heading up the Grand with Pete.

A day after finishing those courses, Steve and I found ourselves hiking up the lower part of the Grand Teton with Pete Athans – heading for a 12 ft. X 18 ft. temporary shelter for the night. And, well before sun-up the next morning, we were awakened, had our breakfast, and started hiking toward the southeast rock wall of the Grand Teton – nervous as wet hens – at 5:15 AM.

The difficulty of our climbing route, the popular Exum Route, varied from easy uphill walking to bouldering, laybacks, and chimneys, to 5.7 – 5.8 technical climbing. Our "route" was mostly not obvious – at all. But with Pete's careful leadership, we made it to the top of the Grand Teton by 10:00 AM – without a clue as to how we were going to get back down. We certainly didn't want to try to climb back down what we had climbed up. And I didn't see any other route. Everything else was spectacularly exposed.

I was looking for a hidden escalator when Pete broke out two climbing ropes, tied them together end-to-end, and tossed one end down the back side of the mountain. He then turned to me and said, "Bill, why don't you go down first." My external self said, "Sure, Pete. I'll be right there." But my internal self said, "Are you kidding me? You want me to go where? You must be crazy!" But I walked up to him cautiously, tied into the rope, closed my eyes, and leaned back. The rest was a haze, but I do recall sliding down the rope (climbers call it rappelling) while I slowly revolved. At one point I recall looking out and thinking to myself, "Holy cow! I think I can see Salt Lake City from here! Whatever am I doing here?" But I did eventually reach the bottom and untied from the rope – on this, a 110 ft. rappel down the Owens-Spalding route - joyous that I was still alive – and didn't have to change my pants!

Once the others were down, Pete came down, recovered the ropes, and immediately came over to me to thank me for going down first. He said, "I sent you down first because I wanted someone at the bottom that I could trust while the others took their turns at rappelling down." That was an unexpected complement.

We enjoyed our hike back to the shelter to recover our gear and on down to the bottom – relieved that, apparently, we had passed the test and were now on our way to Ama Dablam in the famous Himalaya.

October 1992: We flew to Kathmandu, Nepal, via Hong Kong, on Dragon Airlines, after a brief stop in Dhaka, Bangladesh, and checked into our hotel. The front of the hotel had a huge banner tied above its entry way which said:

AMERICAN EXPEDITION AMA DABLAM 1992

That made us feel like real professional mountaineers.

Early the next morning, as I was taking a short walk from the hotel before our planned morning meeting, I encountered a call from across the street in one of those "it's-a-small-world" moments, "Hey Bill! Is that you?" It was Ross Berry from my 1990 Aconcagua Expedition. Following his experience on Aconcagua, he was on some other climbing expedition led by Sergio Fitz-Watkins, the guide that had led my Mt. Elbrus expedition. And, like me, he was offered a spot on Sergio's planned Spring 1992 Mt.

Everest expedition – which he accepted – and went on to summit it (even though Sergio bailed out mid-trip, for some reason, and went home!).

Our Ama Dablam climbing group was a very odd mix of people. In addition to Steve and me, and one other middle-aged client from Boston, it included Al Hanna, an elderly millionaire real estate magnate from Chicago who had lured five other experienced outdoorsmen (rock climbing and white water river guides) into joining his son and him on this trip by paying all of their trip expenses. This was done with the expectation that they join him on his planned climb of Mt. Everest that next spring – again with all expenses paid. And while these five were all very experienced and fit, Al and his son certainly were not. A strange crew it was.

But, following a couple days of organization and packing in Kathmandu, we flew by Twin Otter up to one of the world's highest airport at Lukla at 9,383 ft. elevation – right on the Dudh Kosi River – the main drainage for the south face of Mt. Everest. There all of our packs and gear, once off-loaded from the plane, were loaded onto yaks for the six day trek to our base camp at Ama Dablam. Each night we set up our tents on the grounds of a village tea house where we could order dinner and breakfast. Our six day trek to our base camp allowed us to get acclimatized to the steadily increasing elevation.

When we reached the village of Namche Bazaar at 11,300 ft. we stayed an extra day to do more food shopping in the village market. From here we had our first views of Mt. Everest, Lhotse – and Ama Dablam – off in the distance.

We continued our trek to Deboche after a stop at the famous Tangboche Monastery. At the end of our tour of this famous monastery, the head priest presented each of us with our own white silk kata scarf and then tied a yellow string – with a very special knot – around each of our necks and assured us that, together with his prayers, we would be safe while on the mountain. Later that evening several of our climbers were making light of the apparent silliness of this innocent string. But I didn't fail to notice that at our final farewell dinner in Kathmandu at the end of our trip, not one climber had yet dared to remove his little yellow string.

We continued on the following day to Pangboche at about 13,000 ft.

elevation where we got a tour of the 300 year old gomba, the oldest monastery in the Khumbu region. There were many rock walls along our trail formed by mani stones, or prayer stones, honoring Buddhist traditions. From there we reached our Ama Dablam base camp at about 15,000 ft. where we discovered that we were sharing the mountain with a British team, a Spanish team, a Canadian/Australian team, and two French teams. This was clearly an internationally popular mountain to climb.

Over the next two days we went on day hikes to increasingly higher elevations and then, on our third day there, we all moved up to 17,700 ft. where we established our advanced base camp (ABC). (Over these three days our hired Sherpa men and Sherpani women shuttled our heavier gear up to ABC – saving us a lot of hard work carrying that stuff ourselves.) Steve and I were acclimatizing well and reached camp by 12:30 – with the rest not getting there until 3:00 in the afternoon. Al and his son had a particularly hard time of it. Interestingly, I eventually got sufficiently fit and acclimatized to the point where I could keep up with the Sherpa women as they went uphill – provided that I only had a day pack to carry and they had their typical 60 lb. loads! Keeping up with the load-carrying Sherpa men was easy because they had to stop every half hour or so for a smoke! Temperatures were well below freezing at night, but warmed up nicely once the sun came up. Weather was stable with occasional afternoon snow showers.

October 31st was spent practicing our various roping up techniques and then we made a load carry of some of our personal gear to 19,000 ft. and stashed it before returning to camp. Al, his son, and one other failed to make it to our 19,000 ft. turn-around point.

The next day, November 1st, Todd Burleson, our trip leader, told Steve and me that we'd be on his "A" Team when we eventually head for the summit. That was very comforting. The "B" Team was to be determined by that day's planned climbing. (By implication, there was expected to be a "C" Team – that probably won't get a summit attempt at all.) We climbed that day up to our previous turn-around point at 19,000 ft. where we reached the fixed ropes that had been placed earlier by the Sherpa and Pete to help protect the next steep section. We continued up for another hour or so before turning around to return to ABC.

On our way back down, after stashing our climbing boots, crampons, ice axes and harnesses under a rock, we met up with the second rope team and discovered that one of them, Andy Carson, had been struck on his thigh by a desk-sized rock that had been kicked loose by Al Hanna's son, Brock, who was just ahead of Andy on their rope. The impact broke Andy's right femur and almost knocked him over a 1,000 ft. vertical rock wall. As we waited for the Sherpa to bring up various supplies for the rescue effort, I studied the after-action debris field, but was not able to reconstruct just how this accident occurred. Brock just had to have lunged off the rock in question instead of stepping carefully around the loose rock. He later admitted to me that he had had very little rock climbing experience before coming on this trip – and had certainly not ever climbed the Grand Teton. (Ironically, Andy Carson was the owner of Jackson Hole Mountain Guides, one of only two guide services qualified to lead climbs in the Grand Teton National Park.)

Now our expedition priority moved from climbing to full rescue mode. It took hours and our entire team of climbers and Sherpa to get Andy stabilized and transported back to ABC. Fortunately for us, Todd and Pete were both EMT qualified and we had a considerable stockpile of pharmaceuticals to draw on, but, unfortunately, we were a long way from skilled surgical care.

A young Sherpa boy was immediately dispatched from Base Camp to go to the nearest radio-telephone, which was back at Namche Bazaar, a distance that we covered over three hiking days, to put in a call for helicopter rescue. He ran the entire distance, non-stop, and was there by nightfall. That's when he discovered that the radio-telephone batteries were dead and he was not able to make the call. So, being very resourceful, he went all over the village knocking on doors and borrowing enough batteries to get it working again. Good so far. But then the Nepalese Army personnel would not dispatch one of their helicopters to effect a rescue attempt until they were guaranteed that they would be reimbursed for their efforts.

In anticipation of just such an emergency, Todd had left a cash bond in Kathmandu sufficient to cover just such a flight, but they were not able to identify this bond based on the information that the Sherpa boy had available, and so he, once more, went around town with his hand out borrowing money from one and all to guarantee to the Army that their flight costs would be covered. With that finally in place he then ran, non-stop, back to our Base Camp to insure that we would have our patient ready for transport that next morning.

We awoke early and carried Andy down to an open ridge with a large flat spot suitable for a helicopter landing just below ABC. We estimated that we were at about 17,200 ft. elevation. So far, so good. The helicopter, a French-designed Alouette III, flown by a pilot from the Nepalese Army Air Wing, arrived at Base Camp right at 9:00 AM. Upon learning that our patient was not there, but rather was still up on the mountain at 17,000+ ft., the pilot announced that he could not safely land and take off over 16,000 ft., and so, after lots of fruitless arguing, he turned around and returned to Kathmandu.

We then had no choice but to haul Andy down a very narrow and treacherous trail to Base Camp. Fortunately, the weather was stable, but, unfortunately, we didn't have any sort of litter to use to carry Andy without putting stress on his broken leg. What we wouldn't have given for some sort of rigid stretcher. Everything that we tried to fabricate from tent poles, ropes, tarps and the like just didn't hold up for more than mere minutes, so this trip was as painful for Andy as it was difficult for us working at this elevation. We did manage to recruit climbers and Sherpa from one of the British expeditions and, with their help, reached Base Camp by 3:00 PM – totally worn out.

Once more our young Sherpa ran back out to Namche that same afternoon to make a radio-telephone call to Kathmandu to confirm to the authorities there that our patient had been successfully moved to Base Camp and was ready for evacuation.

The helicopter arrived that next morning at about 8:30 AM and quickly had Andy on his way to a hospital in Kathmandu. But I had forgotten to ask Andy if just maybe he had removed his little yellow string too soon.

At the end of the trip, when we were once more reunited with Andy, we learned that he had been operated on that same day by a Nepalese orthopedic surgeon – who had been trained at the UCLA medical center. Andy was finally in good hands.

Meanwhile back at Base Camp, Pete and Todd assembled a small climbing team to make one single assault on our mountain before packing it in. Their plan was to return to ABC yet that day, climb to Camp 1 up on the side of the mountain the next day, climb to Camp 2 the following day, and make a bid for the summit yet a day later. I was emotionally wasted and took myself out of the running for this climbing effort. Five others offered to join Pete and Todd on this attempt, but eventually three of them turned around well shy of the summit. (The other four did eventually make the summit on this schedule so our expedition was declared a success.)

I joined them on their climb back up to ABC in order to pack out all of my stuff, but Todd wasn't comfortable with me climbing back up to 19,000 ft. where I had left my climbing boots, ice axe, etc. on the day of Andy's accident, because I wouldn't have one of them available to escort me back down to ABC, and they sure didn't need another climbing accident, and so they offered to have one of the Sherpa recover my stuff on their return from the summit.

I was eventually reunited with some of that gear – though my expensive double-plastic climbing boots and crampons somehow got a mind of their own and walked off never to be seen again. That was an expensive loss.

Once Steve had recovered his gear, too, we decided to use the available free days to hike up the Khumbu Valley to Everest Base Camp – only a couple days hike away – to see what that looked like – and mostly to be able to say that we had been there.

On the way that first day we passed a small medical clinic in Pheriche where we saw, leaning up against the building, a classic wire basket litter – the very stiff, light weight stretcher that we would have given a thousand dollars for only a couple days previously. That was so unfortunate. It was so close, and yet we didn't know that it was there.

We spent the night at a tea house in Pheriche at about 14,000 ft. and hiked on the next day to Lobuche (at about 16,200 ft.) which put us within a couple hours of Everest Base Camp. That tea house was very primitive, but still served us excellent French fries, egg omelets, and Sherpa bread. At one point I watched the man of the house bring in a large pile of dried yak dung patties and dropped them beside the oven. He then reached to an upper shelf and brought down a very dirty wedge of cheese and began grating it for use in either my or Steve's cheese omelet. I immediately decided that surely that was for Steve's omelet and moved to a different table so that I wouldn't have to witness how <u>my</u> cheese omelet was made!

That next morning we hiked toward the base camp and then climbed 18,514 ft. Kala Patthar which offered us outstanding views of the entire Everest Base Camp area along with classic views of the famous Icefall, Mt. Everest itself, Lhotse, Nuptse, Chang Tse, Pumori, and many more of the classic Himalayan mountains – all under beautiful blue skies and cold, but stable weather. We figured that our own Ama Dablam climbing team was scheduled to summit that day.

After a second night at the Lobuche tea house, where we were treated with an excellent fresh chocolate layer cake – cooked in a crude stone kiln – using more yak dung for fuel - we headed back down the Khumbu Valley – reuniting with the rest of our team at Deboche. Two more days hiking delivered us back at Lukla where the next morning we caught a flight back to Kathmandu. A couple days later we were all, including Andy, on our way back home after a very exciting, but demanding, exposure to climbing life in the Himalaya.

<u>Postscript:</u> Shortly after Andy got helicoptered out of our Base Camp on Ama Dablam, I rounded up some of the scraps of tent poles and ropes that we had used on his rescue. I also put together a list of every climber, guide, and Sherpa that assisted in our rescue effort. Once home, I made a wooden plaque, attached these rescue scraps, and added a brass plate engraved with the names of everyone who had helped with the rescue. I sent this to Andy at his home in Jackson, Wyoming - along with copies of all of the photos that I had taken during the rescue. He responded with a letter saying how touched he was by this remembrance. Almost a full year later each of us received in the mail from Andy's wife a two inch long ice axe pin of solid silver that she had fabricated in her jewelry shop as her way of showing her appreciation for what we had done to effect his rescue off the mountain. It had taken her nearly that whole year to fabricate enough of them for all of us.

Alps: As of 2002 I had participated in major mountain climbs on six of the seven continents around the world, but had not yet visited the place where the techniques of rock, snow, and ice climbing were first developed. And that was in the famous European Alps. I planned to fix that this year by signing on to a climbing trip to Switzerland and France put together by International Mountain Guides (IMG) and led by Paul Maier and Vince Anderson, both UIAGM internationally certified guides. And once more my good friend, Steve Bridges, agreed to join me on this trip.

After a long flight to Zurich, in August of 2002, followed by a relaxing recovery day, we met up with Paul, our guide, and the other two clients, and drove to Interlochen. Paul warned us on the way that while he has guided this trip six different times, he has very seldom managed to achieve all of the scheduled peaks due to weather problems.

Once in Interlochen we had lunch and then went on to Lautenbrunner where we took a cog rail ride part way up the mountain to Wengen and spent the night under rainy skies. That next morning we took a cog rail further up the mountain to the top station at Jungfraujoch at around 11,300 ft. elevation – stopping half way up to take in views of the north faces of the famous triumvirate: Eiger, Monch, and Jungfrau. (Paul explained that the "job" of the monch ("the monk") is to stand between the eiger ("the oger") and the jungfrau ("the young lady").) Our climbing plan was to attempt to climb the Monch and the Jungfrau. (A different IMG trip includes a climb of the south face of the Eiger.)

Once arriving at the train terminal at Jungfraujoch we explored the observatory, viewing decks, glacier cave, and restaurant before taking a 45 minute trek over to our hut on the slopes of the Monch at about 11,700 ft. elevation. The weather remained totally socked in with temps around freezing. While we did manage to get in some rope technique and ice axe self-arrest training, the continuing bad weather caused us to lose a full day from our plan.

In the meanwhile Vince Anderson, our second guide, showed up and we were now at full strength. As the weather finally cleared late that afternoon, we did manage to get in a short hike up 12,184 ft. Walcherhorn to, again, practice our roped climbing technique.

We were up that next morning at 4 AM and on our way up the Jungfrau in crampons and headlamps by 4:45 AM. Steve and I were on a rope with Vince while the other two were with Paul. Our route was very steep and exposed on lots of fresh snow. At one point I counted 34 climbers on a line behind us, all with the same objective. We were the first to reach the summit at 13,642 ft. at around 9 AM with the weather holding. We kept our summit celebration short because we needed to get off the slopes before the snow got too soft and wet in the sun. And we almost made it. Hiking laterally across our final steep slope we were having to pay particular attention to snow "balling up" on the bottom of our crampons, and so, with each step I was striking each crampon with my ice axe to free up any snow stuck there. But I guess in one case the snow didn't release from one crampon, and when I next placed my weight on that one, it failed to get reliable purchase and I went flying. I did have the foresight to call out "Falling!" to Steve, and he immediately rotated to his left to anchor his ice axe, but the pull of my rope rotated him to his right and immediately we were both sliding down this very steep slope into the abyss. I do recall briefly thinking that I had had a pretty good life up until that point, but never expected that it would end this way, but, oh well, that's the way it was going to be!

And then we both came to an abrupt stop! Vince had worried about the potential for just this sort of thing happening and had secured the rope to an anchor – bringing our slide to a quick stop. What a relief! After a brief pause to collect ourselves, we returned to our original route and finished our traverse much relieved. Once back at the hut, after our eight hour round trip hike, I told Vince that I appreciated that he had saved our lives. He then reminded me that since he was tied into that same rope, he had decided quickly that he had not wanted to join us on our slide to destiny! We also took some time on the way back to patch up Steve since, in our tumble he had managed to spike his left calf with one of the points from his right crampon.

The weather day that we lost cost us an attempt to climb the Monch, and that was a disappointment for sure, but our next objective was very special indeed: Mont Blanc, France and Italy's highest point – as well as being the highpoint of Western Europe at 15,771 ft. elevation.

Once off the mountain Paul drove us all out of Switzerland and into France ending up at the popular ski town of Chamonix. (With there no longer being a need inside EU countries to show one's passport at border crossings, I asked Paul how I would know when we actually entered France. After some thought, he said that that would be easy; just look at the cows. French cows are uglier than Swiss cows!) We got to know Chamonix better than we had planned because the weather deteriorated and we spent a couple days ducking in and out of the rain in town. But, finally, the forecast was for "improving" weather and so we took the telepherique (cable car), just outside of town, up to the top of the Aiquille du Midi ("Middle Peak") at 12,552 ft. elevation. In a complete whiteout and high winds, we hiked across a scary knife-edge ridge to our hut, the Refuge des Cosmiques, with visibility at only four to five feet on very steep terrain in very deep, fresh snow. That was scary, but it put us one step closer to our objective – Mont Blanc.

That next morning the weather was starting to clear, but it was still very windy, so we suited up, roped up, and went for a little "walk" – climbing and traversing all three peaks of nearby Point Lachenal – in 20 to 30 mph winds and gusts well above that. But the sky slowly turned crystal clear with views clear to Mont Rosa and the Matterhorn well inside Switzerland. We made plans to make an attempt on Mont Blanc that next morning. (Paul shared with us his curious observation that in general the average age of clients on guided mountain climbing trips was around 40 while the average age of the guides was around 26. After some thought I told him that that had something to do with the availability of money at those two life points.)

The following morning we were up before 3 AM and on our way by 3:45 AM. By the string of headlamp lights in the distance we could see that that there was already any number of climbing teams on the route that had left one to two hours before us. Once more Steve and I were paired up with Vince while Paul led the other two clients. Within an hour we had caught up with and passed two Japanese teams who had left at 1:00 AM – and then soon passed several other teams as well.

We quickly reached the ridge of the Aiquille du Tacul, dropped into a small basin, and then climbed a very steep wall to Mont Maudit from which we could finally see Mont Blanc itself for the first time. (We later discovered that Paul decided to turn back with his two clients because one of them was slipping too often – creating a serious safety risk.)

Steve and I were pretty exhausted by then and we still had another 3,000 ft. climb in front of us to reach the summit of Mont Blanc, but we persevered. When we finally did make it to the top, we discovered that only one other group had gotten there ahead of us. And we were there well before 10 AM – a six hour ascent of around 5,000 ft. gain. Vince told us that he was very impressed with our fitness for this climb and that made us feel pretty good – especially with me being 60 years of age.

It was still quite windy, but otherwise the weather was stable, and so Vince invited us to get some lunch in us. With tongue in cheek, I told Vince that I was hoping to have lunch in Italy. He gave me a stern look and said, "Don't move!" and he headed a short ways down the south side of the mountain where he quickly cut a small shelf in the snow with his ice axe. Then he invited us to join him, one at a time, still roped up, and sat on this shelf. Then he announced, "You're now in Italy! Have some lunch!" We laughed.

We then descended 6,500 ft. in six hours, on very steep terrain, to a hut where we spent the night – completing our descent the following morning. There were literally hundreds of climbers climbing up that south side hoping to make the summit. We were glad to be heading down. We had just completed the famous Grand Traverse of Mont Blanc.

After more hiking, a telepherique ride, and a cog rail ride, we were finally at the bottom where Paul was waiting with the car and gave us a lift back to Chamonix to reunite with the other two clients.

We drove back into Switzerland – parking the car in Tasch where we then took a cog rail to Zermatt – a totally car-free town. Only electric carts and horse-drawn carriages were permitted on the streets. The famous Matterhorn massive was clearly visible right on the edge of town.

After a restful next morning, we took the tram up the mountain to Rotenbaden in the afternoon from which we hiked to our hut for the night, the Monte Rosa Hut – on the slopes of the Monte Rosa massive,

Switzerland's highpoint at 15,204 ft. elevation (also called Dufourspitze). (The other two clients weren't interested in Monte Rosa and made some other plans for the day.)

That next morning we were up at 2 AM and on the route by 2:45 AM under clear skies. It was a very steep and exposed, but very direct climb to the summit of Monte Rosa – another exhausting 6,000 – 7,000 ft. ascent in 6 ½ hours – arriving shortly after 9 AM. After a short rest, we descended the whole way back to Zermatt that day.

We spent a good part of the following day exploring the Zermatt Alpine Museum where we were surprised to learn that Winston Churchill had climbed Monte Rosa in 1894 and that Theodore Roosevelt had climbed the Matterhorn in 1881.

We took one more long look at the Matterhorn, promised to consider it one day, and began plans to fly back home.

Matterhorn: At the end of our 2002 trip to Switzerland, and especially our several days spent in and around Zermatt, we couldn't take our eyes off the majestic Matterhorn. It looked gigantic, imposing, and intimidatingly difficult. But our guide Vince Anderson told us at the time that we could climb it with the appropriate training. I'm not sure that I believed him at the time, but I did purchase and take home with me a 2 foot by 3 foot photograph of the mountain taken from an angle that fully revealed the northeast (Hornli) ridge containing the most popular summit route. I had told Steve that I was going to frame that photo, hang it above my desk at home, look at it every day, and call him when it no longer intimidated me. And, in August 2004, just two years after our earlier trip, Steve and I were on our way back to Zermatt to make an attempt on the 14,688 ft. Matterhorn.

Once more this trip was organized by International Mountain Guides (IMG) and we were fortunate to again have Vince Anderson as our guide.

He had lined up a whole series of climbs in the area that would allow us to practice climbing on all of the various kinds of rock, ice, and snow that we would encounter on the Matterhorn. For example, even on dry rock we usually practiced climbing with crampons because once on the Matterhorn we could not afford to be taking them on and off at every encounter with snow and ice. In addition to Vince, Steve, and me, our group consisted of two other clients and a second IMG guide, Howie Schwartz.

We started off our training with a day of rock climbing on a dry face of a mountain called the Rifflehorn. We traversed across its top and returned to our hotel for the day. The next day we all took a long hike – ascending over 5,000 ft. – to the Rothern Hut by late afternoon. That set us up for a 5:30 AM wake-up that next morning – leaving the hut by 6 AM to climb the 12,751 ft. Wellenkuppe on mixed snow and rock on a 45 degree slope – returning to the hut by 1:00 PM. From the top we had excellent views of the Matterhorn, Monte Rosa, and the Zinalrothorn.

That afternoon rest was very helpful because we were up at 4 AM and off by 4:30 AM that next morning for a glacier climb of the Zinalrothorn at 13,790 ft. elevation. It turned out to have been a really steep and exposed climb – putting us on top around 11:30 AM. We returned to our hut and continued down the mountain back to Zermatt for a well-earned day of rest.

That rest set us up for a mixed rock and snow climb the following day on the Breithorn (at 13,604 ft. elevation) under, again, very exposed and difficult conditions. We sure were getting a trial by fire (or by ice!).

At this point Vince told us that we now had all of the technical training that we would need to climb the Matterhorn – and, equally important, he would have no reservation about taking us up there – one at a time. That was very reassuring for sure. But he also said that we had to practice one more thing before making the effort. He explained that no matter how early that we tried to start up the Matterhorn, there would be others already on the route. And we would have to practice passing them, quickly, on the climb, or we'd have no hope of making the summit and back in daylight. So that next day we took a bus over to the ski village of Saas Fe, in the next valley, for a climb the following day to the summit of Allalinhorn (13,156 ft.). This peak was chosen because it almost always has a raft of people on its principal route. Once more we were up at 4 AM and on our way by 4:30 AM. And, sure enough, we had plenty of climbers already on the route slowly plodding their way up. We quickly worked our way by all of them and were at the summit by 8:30 AM and back down to Saas Fe for lunch before 11 AM. Now we were fully staged to move up to the Hornli Hut, right at the base of the Hornli Route on the Matterhorn when, overnight, the mountain was hit with a huge snowstorm – stopping all climbing until it melted. What a disappointment to say the least. The snow cover was expected to last at least three days before the mountain could be safely climbed – and neither Steve nor Vince could afford to sit it out for that long. So, after a day to lick our wounds, we made plans to head home – disappointed to say the least.

We talked about coming back one day soon to make a second attempt, but I think we secretly knew that that might never happen – given all of the other places in the world that would be competing for our attention.

Grosglockner: In the summer of 2005 I was offered a wonderful opportunity. Good friends Pete and Carole Feistmann of Tucson were planning to spend a month or two in Eastern Europe in the fall. And they invited me to join them for the first week or two of their trip. These couple weeks were to be spent around Lienz, Austria – cycling and hiking. Never having been there, I was thrilled to accept their kind invitation to join them. But the real icing on the cake was when Pete announced that he had plans to include, during that same period, a two day climb of the Grosglockner, Austria's highest mountain at 12,461 ft. elevation – complete with trained guides. I packed up my bike – climbing boots and harness, crampons, and ice axe – and flew over there in early September.

After arriving in Lienz and getting settled in, Pete put together a series of cycling days in and around Lienz that varied from dead flat one day to 3,000 ft. climbs of 15 – 20% grades on the other days. I recall making it up one incredibly steep grade simply because I didn't think I could stop the bike and get off without falling over! I did manage to stay with Pete on the way up these steep grades, but neither one of us was setting any speed records. Fortunately, there was a ski lodge at or near the top of every climb – serving ice cold radler drinks – a beer /lemonade combination that really hit the spot. Carole's favorite riding day was when we rode a flat stretch of bike trail for some 55 miles along the river, stopped for lunch, and took the train back to Lienz. (Secretly, Pete and I liked that day, too.)

But then, following a day of sightseeing, we drove to nearby Kals to begin our mountain climb up the Grosglockner. We were joined there by Hans Oberlohr, Pete's close friend from Vail, Colorado – who was raised in Kals and, years earlier, used to guide climbers on the Grosglockner. Also joining us were two of Han's friends from the USA: Johnny Meuller and Phil Patman.

Our first rest stop on the way up the mountain was at Lucknerhutte, the first of several mountain huts – offering food, drinks, and lodging. Our second stop was for lunch at the Studlhutte hut where we met up with Hans Rogl, a paid mountain guide. Rogl passed out the crampons, ice axes, and climbing harnesses to Johnny, Phil, Pete, and Carole. Hans Oberlohr and I had our own climbing equipment.

Shortly after lunch Hans Rogl had his team all harnessed and roped up and headed up and across a large glacier field leaving Hans Oberlohr and me to sort out how we were going to travel. Hans took the lead initially and I tied in right behind him on his rope and we, too, were soon off across the glacier. But almost immediately Hans began quizzing me on where I might have climbed before, and so I admitted to having climbed Mt. McKinley in Alaska. He liked hearing that and immediately asked if I had climbed anywhere else. I truly wanted to avoid anything that sounded like bragging. But I did admit to having climbed once in Argentina – on Aconcagua. That seemed to impress him and so he quietly continued this interrogation. And when I told him of having climbed some in the Swiss Alps, he stopped, turned around, starred at me for a moment, and quietly untied his rope.   He then handed me the end of the rope and moved around behind me saying, "Heck, you're better trained at this than I am! You lead from here!" We had a good laugh over that, but from then on he insisted that I lead our 2-man rope team. That made me nervous because I really had no idea what was in store for us further up the mountain.

At the end of the glacier field we reached a very steep, rocky ridge that we had to ascend. It was quite steep, but there were, here and there, steel bars to help provide secure hand and foot holds, and we were soon up and over this obstacle and arrived at the third and final hut, the Adlerstrule ("Eagles Roost"), where we were to spend the night.

During all of this the weather remained dry, but unsettled. And when we got up that next morning we discovered that we had received an inch or so of fresh snow overnight. None-the-less, the sky was clearing to a bright blue and we were stoked to finish the final ¾ mile climb from our hut to the summit. Carole decided that she wasn't fond of the new, slippery snow and opted to stay at the hut awaiting our return, but the other five of us all tied into Hans Rogl's rope and headed for the summit. The terrain wasn't especially difficult, but the fresh snow made it quite slippery, and the exposure was often very severe. In due time we all successfully summited – feeling great about our accomplishment. Along the way we also climbed the Kleinglockner at 12,411 ft. elevation, a lesser peak of the Grosglockner and Austria's third highest mountain.

After taking exactly two bazillion photos on top, we gingerly reversed our steps and returned to the Adlerstrule hut. The hut caretaker, upon hearing of our summit success, broke out a bottle of schnapps and we all had a toast to our success. With care we retraced our steps back down the rocky ridge and across the glacier field to the Studlhutte hut where the climbers all turned in their harnesses, ice axes, and crampons – and said our goodbyes to Hans Rogl. The hut proprietor, upon hearing of our climbing success, broke out the schnapps and we all had a shot to celebrate, once more, our success.

Once back on the trail, we made a brief stop at the first hut, the Lucknerhutte, and, you guessed it, celebrated with yet again another shot of schnapps.

At the bottom, at the parking lot, Hans announced that we were invited to stop by his sister's place in Kals for coffee, soup, rolls, deserts, and, yes, some more schnapps. I was glad that I wasn't in charge of driving back to Lienz. It was a truly great day with wonderful friends.

After a well-earned recovery day and a wonderful day hike with Pete and Carole up the nearby Zettersfeld, I made plans to return home with a huge sense of fulfillment.

South America

Patagonia: While I had been climbing in both the Himalayas and the Alps since, I had not been back to South America in over 10 years. And so in 2003 I signed up for a mountaineering expedition to the Patagonia region of Argentina. This trip was put together by the esteemed American Alpine Institute with a plan to attempt climbs on four peaks in Patagonia's famous Cerro Torre / Fitzroy area. This region includes some of the hardest mountain climbs in the world – especially when considering the often violent and highly unpredictable weather that goes with this part of the world, so we were told to look to this trip as more of a trek with some very modest mountain climbing thrown in rather than strictly as a climbing expedition. I was OK with that. (Patagonia is located around 50 degrees south latitude, further south than Australia, New Zealand, or the southern tip of Africa, and so the prevailing winds out of the west at this latitude have traveled the whole way around the world without interruption before slamming into the Andes of southern South America. As a result, weather on the eastern slopes of this range is often turbulent, severe, quick changing, and totally unpredictable.) While I was looking forward to trying my hand at some real climbing, I was also looking forward to seeing some of the rest of the glaciers, high plains, and serious mountains of Patagonia, too.

We flew directly from the states to Santiago and on to Punta Arenas, the southern most commercial airport in Chile (and in South America). While on our trip across these plains in Chile and on into Argentina, we got to see plenty of ostrich-like birds called lesser rhias, llamas, and guanacos. We stopped overnight at Calafate, a quaint tourist town with plenty of cabanas and tourist shops. From here we were able to see close up the popular Moreno Glacier and watched it calf into the surrounding lake.

After visiting the glacier, we drove on to El Chalten where we arranged for some horses to carry our duffels in to the interior. El Chalten looked a lot like a raw frontier town whose only purpose in life was to provide a rough and tumble destination for serious mountain climbers. We started our hike into the interior – in steady rain – to Bridwell Camp for the night, right near the base of the famous Cerro Torre peak. Our horse pack train consisted of two sets of four horses each. The first set went to the wrong camp miles from where we were and the second set, while arriving at the correct camp, arrived three hours late. We were off to a great start! We finally got everything together and camp set up – in the dark – in the rain – by 9 PM and had dinner at 10 PM – by flashlight. Turned in at 11 PM.

Our travel group consisted of 27 year old head guide, Dylan Taylor, his 24 year old assistant, Derek Elliott, and eight clients: two from British Columbia, one from Alaska, one from Utah, and my good friend, Steve Bridges, and me from Arizona. Bridwell Camp consisted of a large number of tents, in the middle of a small forest, housing both tourists as well as serious mountain climbers. Dylan and Derek had already been in the high peaks region for many weeks already and managed to get up some really serious climbing routes in the Cerro Torre range. We thought we were in good hands.

The next day we ventured out onto the Torre Glacier for some crampon practice. (Some of the clients had never even seen crampons before! This didn't bode well for our future climbing success.) To get to the glacier we had to first cross the raging Rio Fitzroy at the glacier lake's outlet. Someone previously had strung a strong climbing rope across the river and so we used it to get across using a technique called a Tyrolean Traverse where you clip the rope onto your climbing harness, swing your feet up and over the rope, and use your arms to pull yourself across the river – often only a few feet above the raging river. Again, many in our group had never experienced that before and managed to get soaking wet in the process. It rained off and on all day long, too, just to add to our discomfort. Though we were only a few hundred yards from the famous Cerro Torre Peak itself, the cloud bank completely obscured our view of it.

The following day our itinerary called for us to make an attempt on Cerro Solo. It was only a short distance from camp. While not really all that high at 7373 ft. elevation, it should have provided us with outstanding views of the overall Torre Valley that we were in. But instead, we packed up and hiked east to Camp Poincenot just off the east face of Fitzroy. When I asked Dylan about Cerro Solo, he said that he didn't even know that our itinerary included it! Strike one!

Once more we set up camp in the middle of a birch forest so that we'd have something of a windbreak from the never ending winds. We surrounded our tent with logs and tree branches to further break the wind. Here we were scheduled to make an attempt that next morning on Cerro Valluda at 6439 ft. right in front of Fitzroy's famous southeast face. But this, too, was not to be. A park ranger discovered that there was something seriously wrong with our permit and we couldn't attempt any climbs until that was straightened out. Strike two!

Early that following morning Dylan hiked back to El Chalten, where there was a telephone, to get our permit issue fixed. For some odd reason he took Derek with him. We were left alone. Strike three! Steve and I went exploring – until the rain returned and then we hid out in our tent. Dinner that night awaited Dylan and Derek's return – well after dark.

During that day a small group of Japanese photographers came into camp by horseback and immediately set up their cameras in an adjacent clearing in order to photograph the famous Fitzroy Mountain. They immediately began taking many, many photographs using a large variety of lenses, light filters, and film speeds. Several of the photographers even had assistants to help them with all of this gear. This went on until dark and commenced again early that next morning up until their horses returned and they had to leave.

What made this simply hilarious to us all was that at no time in all of this was even a tiny piece of Fitzroy visible at all. There was not even so much as an outline visible through the persistent cloud bank. I have to wonder what they did with all of those hundreds of photographs – of a cloud bank. Of course, as luck would have it, twenty minutes after they left, the cloud bank totally dissipated and we were left with an outstanding view of the entire mountain.

The next morning we were up at 5 AM to try our hand at climbing Cerro Velluda at 6439 ft. – hoping for magnificent views of Fitzroy. But with high winds, light rain, and snow higher up, that was ultimately cancelled. We went back to bed and got up later for a long hike instead.

That evening, at sunset, we had another complete view of Fitzroy – lit by the setting sun. It was striking. The high winds remained with us. This was getting old.

Our pack horses showed up early that next morning to haul our gear to what would be our third and final camp: Piedra del Fraile – a privately run concession complete with toilets, a shower, and cold beer – and excellent views of Fitzroy and other nearby peaks. We were to stay here for the next four days before returning to El Chalten. Things were looking up – we thought.

The next morning we were up at 5 AM and on the trail by 6 AM under clear skies and only moderate winds. We hiked to the Marconi Glacier by 9:30 AM and up to the Marconi Pass by noon – intending on making a bid on Cerro Marconi Norte's summit. But Dylan decided that we had not moved up the glacier fast enough and therefore didn't have enough time to make the summit and still be back to camp before dark. So our attempt was abandoned and we headed back to camp from there. Strike four! Certainly a contributing problem was that a couple of the clients were really not very fit and had moved very slowly up the glacier. But we had also been delayed by a client who wasn't paying attention and stepped into a crevasse. He was carrying one of our two climbing ropes. Interestingly, the first person to his aid was another one of the clients who ran right up to the edge of the crevasse to try to help him – with the other of our two ropes. Had he gone in, too, we wouldn't have had a rope to use for a rescue! The guides had not provided any instructions or warning regarding the crevasse risk. And we weren't roped up. I thought that the crevasse risk was really minimal, but then I had been exposed to them before and knew what to watch for. We returned to camp disappointed, in high winds and more rain, for a twelve hour day on the ice pursuing a plan that was doomed from the start.

Tomorrow's plan was to make an attempt on our fourth planned climb, Punta Fina. But that wasn't to be either what with more very high winds and on again / off again rain. We tried several times to go on short walks away from camp, but even then the wind was simply too strong to stand up safely.

In the evening our camp host roasted a whole lamb over an open fire just for us and served it together with potatoes, yams, and fresh made bread. We ate like ravenous cavemen.

On our final day in the interior we were, again, up at 5:00 AM and on the way by 6:00 AM to make a second attempt on Punta Fina despite still experiencing very high winds and rain. Part way up the rain turned to sleet and then to snow, but we all agreed to press on anyway – except for the guides – who were campaigning to cash it in and split. They just weren't motivated, and it showed, but we wouldn't let them off the hook without a serious attempt to summit at least this one peak.

We eventually reached a long icefield just below the summit at about 11,000 ft. elevation where, in better weather, we could have summited in 20 minutes or so. But with wind gusts requiring us to hug large rocks to keep from getting blown off the mountain, we ducked behind a rock wall, took a snack break, declared success, and headed back down the mountain – exuberant that we had finally gotten in at least a little bit of serious climbing.

Late breakfast that next morning; broke camp in the rain (What else?), and walked out to the road where we got a taxi back to El Chalten for dinner and a night's rest in a hotel there. Next day was a very long drive back to Punta Arenas for our flights out of Chile. I couldn't help but notice that end-of-trip tips for Dylan and Derek were in very short supply.

POSTSCRIPT: Some of the clients must have complained formally to Dunham Gooding, Director of American Alpine Institute, because he personally interviewed every one of us and then, sometime later, wrote us all a formal letter of apology for how badly this trip was run. He explained that Derek had been fired, Dylan was demoted, and all of us got a check for $250 and a $250 credit for use on a future expedition. Now that was totally unexpected.

Ecuador: Two years after my "climbing" trip to Patagonia, I was off to Quito, Ecuador in December 2005 on another climbing adventure, again with American Alpine Institute. My son Scott joined me on this one. Our base plan was to climb, over a two week period, five significant peaks, all extinct volcanoes.

Our team consisted of American guides Andy Wexler and his sidekick Joey Elton, an Ecuadorian guide Rene Floress, and ten of us clients. After a day touring around the popular Otovalo Market in Quito so that we could leave as much of our money in the economy as possible, we went on an acclimatization climb up Cerro Pasochoa at 13,776 ft. elevation. This long walk went through a beautiful forest preserve. We celebrated this fine long walk with evening dinner in Quito's tourist district – called "Gringolandia" by the locals.

Most of us were surprised to discover that some years ago Ecuador had abandoned their peso-based currency and adopted American money. Ever wonder what happened to all of those Susan B. Anthony and Sacagawea dollar coins? They are in circulation in Ecuador in lieu of one dollar bills.

The next day, continuing our acclimatization program, we hiked up a peak called Gua Gua Pichincho at 15,728 ft. elevation and then over-nighted in the vintage Hacienda Guachola dating from the 1500's. It was a very impressive place, but had no central heat. We froze. I guess that, too, was part of our acclimatization.

Now we could start getting serious about climbing. In the morning we drove and hiked up to a hiker's hut at 15,250 ft. elevation on the flanks of 18,993 ft. Cayambe, an old volcano. We spent a full day there practicing jumaring (climbing) up a fixed rope, walking and climbing on glacier ice with crampons and ice axes, and other such skills. We turned in early only to be awakened at midnight for a quick breakfast and on our way up the mountain by headlamps shortly after 1 AM.

We were organized into three rope teams – each led by one of our three guides. At about two hours into our climb three of our clients weren't feeling well and opted to turn back. They did so with one of the guides while the rest of us reorganized into two rope teams and continued on toward the summit – reaching it about 8:30 AM shortly after sun up. Unfortunately some sort of storm front was moving in and we didn't see anything from the top. We were back at the hut before noon completely exhausted. Little did we know that that was going to turn out to be our first and last of the planned big climbs for the trip. We packed up and headed back to the Hacienda Guachola for some good rest. Two days later, on Christmas Eve, after more resting and driving, we entered Cotopaxi National Park and reached 15,100 ft. elevation by bus and 15,729 ft. on foot to the Ribas Hut on the flanks of 19,347 ft. Cotopaxi, another volcano – with plans to climb it that night. It had been raining and snowing all day – not ideal conditions for a climb on steep slopes. None the less, we were up at 12:30 AM and on our way up the mountain by 1:30 AM. After a few hours Joey and Rene stopped for an extended pow wow and concluded that we were climbing on wind slab snow that was in immediate danger of avalanching. Disappointed as we were, we high-tailed it back down the mountain and got safely back to the climber's hut in one piece. The mountain won that one! We drove to Hacienda San Agustin – a ranch built on the site of the northern most Inca ruins known – for lunch.

Following that, we drove further south to Estacion Urbina, an old train station, and right at the base of Chimborazo, our next target volcano to climb – the highest mountain in Ecuador at 20,702 ft. elevation. It rained off and on all morning long and then turned to steady rain in the afternoon. But with all of this rain – which was all snow higher up on the mountain – there was no reason to believe that it would be safe to climb either. Bummer.

After dragging our feet here for another day and not seeing any improvement in the weather, we turned back north and drove to El Chaupi as a sort of consolation effort. On foot, with horses carrying our gear, we hiked up to a climber's cabin for the night on the side of Illiniza and, early that next morning, managed to ascend Illiniza's North Peak at 16,794 ft. elevation in about three hours. That was quick enough for us to get back down off the mountain in time to drive to Termas Papallacta where there was a wonderful pool and hot springs to enjoy – in the rain, of course. We had just experienced 15 days of near continuous rain. As disappointed as I was in not gaining more high summits, my overall experience with Ecuador was positive and I promised myself that I would return for a second try at those missed peaks. And, besides, I was fortunate enough to have gotten to know our Ecuadorian guide, Rene Floress, who I could deal with directly for a future trip.

Ecuador II: Two years later, in January 2007, I returned to Ecuador. I had been in touch with Rene Floress, one of our guides from my effort there in 2005. He had put together a plan to make a second attempt on those missed peaks from my 2005 expedition.

I contacted all of the clients from our 2005 effort to see if any of them wanted to join me, but only got one taker – Teresa Gergens from Denver. Teresa was small of frame, but was a serious "peak bagger" that few could equal. She had already climbed all 58 of Colorado's 14,000 ft. peaks as well as all 637 of the state's 13,000 ft. peaks and was already well on her way to be the first to climb all of the 12,000 ft. and 11,000 ft. peaks as well. Talk about being driven, obsessed – and more than a little crazy!

Upon flying in to Quito we met up with Rene, who led us on a couple acclimatization hikes, including nearby Pasochoa, and another dinner in "Gringolandia," before heading once more to El Chaupi for our hike back up to the climber's hut on the flanks of Illiniza. There we ran into a climbing group from Mountain Madness – among a number of others. Fortunately for us, most of them were headed for Illiniza Norte in the morning while we were going to try our hand at its much higher and steeper neighbor Illiniza Sur (Illiniza South) at 17,300 ft. elevation. Up at 1:30 AM and on our way by 2:30 AM by headlamps on a route that was continuously steep – up to 70% in places - in solid snow and ice clear to the summit – with almost no place to stop for a break. We reached the top, totally wasted, by 7:00 AM in bright sunlight with outstanding views of many of the other peaks on our agenda. The snow conditions were far from ideal so we didn't stick around very long, but beat feet quickly back to our hut and back down to El Chaupi.

After lunch we drove to La Estacion de Machachi for a day of rest – followed the next day by a visit to the impressive Quilotoa Crater Lake.

Then we drove to the Cotopaxi National Park's Jose Ribas Hut in preparation for our second attempt to climb up the Cotopaxi volcano. We were enjoying stable weather so we had great hopes for a successful climb this time.

We were up at 11 PM and on the trail by midnight in excellent snow and very little wind for this attempt. We reached the top, at 19,348 ft. elevation, before 6:00 AM as the sun rose, and were back to the hut in less than two hours, and on to the Hosteria La Cienega for the night. They had hot water for a shower, but only for a minute or two at a time, which made showering a challenge.

We spent the next day touring in the hot and humid village of Banos, a serious tourist town right on the edge of the tropical rain forest. That certainly warmed us up. Rene's friend Miguel was our guide as we hiked to three beautiful waterfalls in the area. Banos was right at base of one of the very few active volcanoes in Ecuador. (Many of the workers kept a wide board handy to hold over their heads to protect them from falling rocks while walking to work when the volcano was erupting.)

The next day we drove, with Miguel, to Ambato for lunch, where we met up with Rene, and continued our drive to a hiker's hut at 15,800 ft. low on the slopes of Chimborazo – our next targeted volcano climb. Chimborazo, at 20,800 ft. elevation is the highest mountain in Ecuador and at one point many years ago was thought to be the highest mountain in the world.

On the drive to the mountain we saw domesticated alpaca and, on the flanks of Chimborazo, lots of the relatively rare vicuna. There we came to understand that Miguel was going to climb with us in the morning. Rene was concerned that Teresa's hiking pace might slow me down and cause me to get too cold to continue the climb. So now we'd each be roped to our very own guide up the mountain! Now that's service – at no extra charge. But it did surprise me because Teresa's hiking pace had been every bit as fast as mine all along.

The plan for Chimborazo was to climb up from the hiker's hut to a temporary tent camp on a moraine at about 17,550 ft. on the first day. We would then attempt to summit the following day and return the whole way back to the hiker's hut. We would have porters to haul our overnight gear and tents to this temporary moraine camp and recover it all a day later so that we could concentrate exclusively on our climbing.

It took us only four hours to hike up to this camp and set up the tents for the night. This portion of the route was all rock, gravel, and sand almost the entire way.

We were up shortly after midnight and quickly on our way up the mountain. Our terrain quickly changed from rock to sheer ice and snow and was also very steep. That was tricky, but it soon changed to just snow and that helped a lot with traction even though still steep. We reached the Ventimilla, the "first" top, right at sunrise. Happily, the weather, while very cold, was still clear and holding, and, to Teresa's delight, we agreed to continue hiking over to the very slightly higher Whymper Summit.

We hiked back down to the moraine camp and on to the hiker's hut to retrieve our gear and drove on to Ambato for lunch and then back to Quito.

Our original plan had been to try to climb 18,891 ft. Antisana as our final peak, but Rene had not been able to find any climbers who had managed to navigate across its massive bergschrund, so we were forced to reevaluate our plan. (A bergschrund is a special ice/snow crevasse that forms right against the steep slope of a mountain.)

We spent our rest day at the hot spring/pool in Papallacta – together with Patricia Serrano, the office manager for Mountain Legends, Rene's employer. The following day we had a fairly relaxing day taking the aerial cable car to a high ridge overlooking Quito and then with Marcel, our stand-in guide, we did a rock climb to the top of Ruca Pichinia at 15,430 ft. in fog and hail – returning by a much easier route. This was a special treat because Marcel was the current president of the Ecuadorian Mountain Guide Association – and a really nice guy.

We spent our final day in Quito touring Ecuador's grand monument to the equator. It is very elaborate, but, unfortunately, modern-day GPS's reveal that it is actually a good ways away from the Earth's actual equator.

Bolivia: I was so pleased overall with my 2007 Ecuador climbing trip with Rene Floress and Mountain Legends that I asked them to propose a climbing trip to Bolivia in 2008. So, in August of that year I found myself flying into the La Paz airport at sun-up where Rene was waiting for me. The story often told is that this airport is the only place where airline pilots put on oxygen masks <u>after</u> landing because of its elevation of 13,390 ft. above sea level. The airport is located high on the altiplano with La Paz, the capital city spread 1,500 ft. down through a huge canyon – with the poorer people living high in this canyon and the more well off folks living well down into the canyon – closer to the start of the rain forest.

After a strange shower that was first lukewarm, then very hot, and finally ice cold (!), we took a tour around town – with special attention to the "Witches Market." Here we saw lots of very strange things for sale – including, of all things, llama fetuses which were to be hung at the doorway entrance to ones house for good luck!!! Wow! Some good luck charm!

For the next day's acclimatization hike, we drove to an old abandoned ski center at 16,000 ft. and hiked up to 17,800 ft. That sure speeded up our acclimatization! From there we had an excellent view of Huayna Potosi, a peak that we would be attempting later in our trip. To my dismay, my camera started misbehaving and soon was useless. That was a disappointment, to say the least, because we were in some very impressive mountain country.

The following morning we took a taxi for a 2 – 3 hour drive across the altiplano to a remote access trail to the Condiriri Base Camp. There we met up with a lady packer and her five burros who hauled our gear to camp in a cirque of 16,000 and 17,000 ft. peaks. We saw herds of llamas everywhere. Joining us also was Eulogio, a local from Le Paz, who was going to act as our base camp manager and cook while we were camped there.

A day later we climbed nearby Cerro Vintannani at 17,845 ft. elevation for acclimatization and on the following day we practiced our knots, roping techniques, and crevasse rescue high up on the glacier in preparation for our upcoming big climb. That afternoon I snuck off without telling Rene and climbed Pica Mirador at 17,325 ft. in a quick three hours.

That next day we were up at 2:30 AM and on the trail by 3:30 AM to make an attempt on Pequeno Alpamayo – a nearby icy peak, named after the more famous Alpamayo Peak in Peru. It involved a climb up a long, narrow, and steep ridge. It was very exciting climbing. We summited, in clear, stable weather, by mid-morning, and were back in camp by 12:30 PM totally exhausted.

At camp Eulogio told me that, as a reward for our success, he would fix me anything that I wanted for lunch. Not believing him, I asked for a llama cheeseburger and French fries plus a cold beer. He never flinched as he turned and walked away. A very short while later he called me to lunch: a cheese burger (which he swore was llama), fries, and a cold beer awaited! I was shocked. I have no idea how he pulled that off, but he did. And it really hit the spot.

Later that afternoon, after a nice nap, Eulogio again approached me and asked what I wanted for dinner. And, again, didn't tell me what my choices were. So, seeing a glacier-fed lake nearby, I told him I'd like fresh trout and cold beer for dinner. And, with no idea how he did it, we had a huge, freshly baked trout for dinner – and more cold beer. What a pleasant surprise. This meal was complemented with more French fries, mashed potatoes, and dried and fried bananas.

We hiked back out to the road in the morning, once the burros returned, and called for a taxi to drive us back to La Paz for a day of rest. I used my rest day to take a guided tour of the nearby Tiwanaku archeology ruins and museum. I had a llama steak for dinner.

The next day we taxied again for a couple hours out of Le Paz to the trailhead for 19,890 ft. Huayna Potosi, one of the highest peaks in Bolivia. Eulogio joined us once again. We were met there by two very young boys who appeared out of thin air to help carry our loads up the mountain. We hiked right up to the snow line at Rock Camp at about 17,200 ft., where we made camp for the night. The weather was very stable with very few clouds – a good omen for our night time climb to come.

We were up at 2 AM and on the route to the summit by 3 AM – reaching it at just after 7 AM – for a 4 hour ascent time. (Rene said that his previous climbs averaged 5 – 6 hours one way, so that made me feel good.) There were plenty of huge crevasses along the way, but they were all easy to see – and avoid. The final third of the climb was on a very steep, knife-edged ridge on very old snow. We were back to our Rock Camp by 9:30 AM for a round trip time of only 6 ½ hours. After a short rest (and some hot soup) we were back at the bottom of the mountain at the trailhead by 11 AM and back in La Paz by 1:30 PM – totally worn out.

Our original plan had been to attempt a climb up Parinacota, but an impending nation-wide labor strike caused us to scratch that part of our expedition and head back home immediately. We left in the morning following an overall very satisfying exposure to Bolivia.

Peru: Early in 2012 I felt that I was ready for yet another international mountain climbing trip and I hadn't yet been to Peru. And while I really didn't know of any particular mountains that I wanted to climb there, except for one called Alpamayo, I knew that in the Cordillera Blanca range alone there were hundreds of candidate high peaks. And so I once more contacted Rene Floress and Mountain Legends to have them propose an agenda that included Alpamayo and recommend a good time to climb them.

As mentioned elsewhere here, Alpamayo was one of four "magical" mountains world-wide that had a particularly classical pyramidal shape that mountaineers especially appreciate. I had already attempted to climb one of them, Ama Dablam in Nepal, that got aborted due to an unfortunate climbing accident. I had made an attempt on a second mountain in this quartet – the famous Matterhorn in Switzerland – but got turned back due to an unexpected snow storm – in August. Now I was hoping for success on Alpamayo. Beyond that, and not being familiar with Peru's mountains, I wasn't particular as to what else we climbed.

I received a climbing proposal from Mountain Legends that interested me, and in July 2012 I found myself in Huarez, Peru, by way of Lima, where I met up with Rene Floress and his partner Mauricio Beltran. Only then did Rene reveal that he was still recovering from a serious climbing accident the previous year and had brought along Mauricio to take the lead in any serious climbing that we were to take on. Mauricio and I hit it off well right from the start, so that was good. We had fun touring a local market where we could buy live chickens, rabbits, and cuy (guinea pigs – a delicacy in Peru) for dinner if we'd like. I chastised Rene for not planning to have cuy for our meals high on the mountain.

We spent the first couple days once more acclimatizing to higher elevations by hiking to a hidden lake, Laguna Churup, at 14,680 ft. elevation and exploring the Willkawain Archeological Monument before heading to the trailhead to the Mt. Pisco Refugio. This hiker's retreat was already at 15,444 ft. elevation with a variety of peaks spread before it, or so I was told, because we were enveloped in thick fog the entire time. That was supposed to be very unusual for this time of year. With full porter support, after over-nighting at the refugio, we hiked up to a camp on a glacial moraine at about 16,200 ft. elevation. Unfortunately, my pack, tent, and ice tools ended up someplace else. That generated some consternation, but we eventually discovered them another 1,000 ft. higher up on the moraine.

We spent a cold night at this moraine camp only to awake to more heavy fog making an ascent of Mt. Pisco totally out of the picture. A couple coming down the trail to our camp reported that they had had to abandon their summit attempt because of the thick, enveloping fog making their route finding impossible. So, after dragging our feet for a time, we hoofed it back to the refugio, waited for a porter to recover our gear, and headed back down to the trailhead for a lift back to Huarez. I have no idea why we didn't stick around for a day or two to see if this fog would lift.

Along the way down Rene learned that Alpamayo was not safely climbable due to some serious snow problem at the bottom of the peak. Another disappointment. Welcome to the real world of high altitude mountain climbing.

This left me in a bit of a quandary. How should I pick the next peak (or peaks) to attempt. I realized that we'd not likely make a second attempt on Mt. Pisco and Alpamayo was now not available either. I knew that, given a choice, I'd opt for whatever was the highest available, but I wasn't driven to choose an especially hard one since it really wouldn't mean much to anyone back home – or even to me either.

This quandary of what to choose never left me. For the first time in all my years I was faced with having to try to get enthusiastic about a climb that really didn't mean anything special to me. Every mountain that I had climbed up to that point was either on my special goal list or was in preparation for one to follow that was. Maybe I had not done enough homework before planning for my Peru trip.

We went back to Huarez for dinner and some regrouping. The following day Rene left to return to Ecuador confident that Mauricio and I would get along fine together. We drove to another beautiful mountain valley in Huascaran National Park and contracted to have our duffels hauled by burros to the Ishinca Refugio. We hiked in right behind them. This turned out to be a very popular way station with climbers tented all around the hut. We got a room in the refugio itself with ready access to toilets, showers, a kitchen, fire place, and cold beer.

That following morning, again with full porter support, we hiked to a high camp on the flanks of Ischinca Mountain – where, at 2 AM that next morning we climbed by headlamp in steep snow and ice to Ishinca's summit at 18,579 ft. elevation – arriving there before 6 AM that morning – right at sunrise. There were literally dozens and dozens of snow-covered high altitude peaks all around us. We were back to our camp and back at the refugio before noon with a well-earned peak to our credit.

After a day of rest our plan was to repeat this very same sequence on the slopes of neighboring Tocllaraju – with a high camp at 16,681 ft. elevation. Now this peak was really impressive – with very steep, crevasse-filled slope to the summit – in full view of our camp.

We made it up to our high camp by the middle of the afternoon so we had plenty of time to obsess over the mountain slope still above us. We turned in as soon as the sun set.

Here I was in a tent high on the flanks of a really scary-steep, ice and snow-covered mountain with a name I couldn't remember – or pronounce – that I'd never heard of before – with no company except a guide – in another tent – who struggled to speak English – located a zillion miles from nowhere – all by myself - with no idea what I was doing there. Talk about having an existential moment! I had the very distinct feeling that this might very well be my last really high altitude climb.

I slept lightly and was up at 1:30 AM for a 2:30 AM departure, fully suited up with plastic boots, crampons, ice axe and headlamp – roped up for the ascent. It was good to get going because it was bitterly cold.

During one of our brief breaks, I spied two dots of light high up on the mountain that I was sure were two climbers well ahead of us. I was also sure that before sun-up we'd catch up to them, but at each rest stop they looked to still be well ahead of us. It wasn't until the very earliest crack of dawn when I could start to make out the outline of the peak in front of us, that I realized that those two "climbers" were actually two stars! No wonder I wasn't gaining on them! We didn't reach the summit at 19,912 ft. elevation until 9:40 AM because of difficulty crossing several exposed and deep crevasses – in the dark.

The views from the top were spectacular. We found ourselves nearly surrounded by dozens and dozens of snow-covered peaks glimmering in the morning sun up and down the range of the Cordillera Blanca. We stayed on top until the cold forced us to get moving again and then we headed down – reaching our high camp by 2 PM. We continued down to the refugio that same afternoon.

A shower and dinner, a good night's sleep, and a three hour hike that next morning got us back to the trailhead for our drive back to Huarez and our return to civilization – still reveling in our Ishinca / Tocllaraju duo accomplishment. I left Peru with good feelings overall – glad that I had had a chance to experience climbing in some of Peru's highest mountains and still wondering if just maybe I had finally satiated my drive for high altitude mountaineering.

Mt. McKinley Base Camp, Alaska

Mt. McKinley Camp 6, Alaska

Pico de Orizaba, Mexico

On summit of Aconcagua, Argentina

Mt. Kilimanjaro, Tanzania

With Scott on Mt. Kilimanjaro, Tanzania

Zebras, Serengeti Game Reserve, Tanzania

Mt. Elbrus, Russia

Carstensz Pyramid, New Guinea

With natives near Carstensz Pyramid, New Guinea

Flying to Antarctica

With Scott on Mt. Vinson Summit, Antarctica

Mt. Rainier, Washington

Ama Dablam, Nepal

Borland in Shigatse, Tibet

Mt. Everest (North Side), Tibet

Mt. Everest (South Side), Nepal

Alps, Switzerland

Borland on Grossglockner Summit, Austria

Crossing River, Patagonia, Argentina

Patagonia, Argentina

Borland on Summit of Cotopaxi, Ecuador

Borland on Summit of Picino Alpamayo, Bolivia

Tocllaraju, Peru

Borland on Summit of Tocllaraju, Peru

Borland in Phu Bai, Vietnam

Borland on Mt. Fuji, Japan

Chapter Five

White Water Rafting

Middle Fork of the Salmon

In the nine years that I lived in New York State, I managed to get in, literally, thousands of river miles in a canoe or kayak on weekend and week-long trips on various rivers and lakes in New York, Pennsylvania, New England, and eastern Canada. Each spring we looked for normally quiet, gentle streams that would be roaring with snow run off – and in the summer, rivers that would provide navigable waterways for two and three day weekend canoe camping trips. And while these rivers, as a general rule, wouldn't compete with high volume water found in big rivers in the west, they did teach us how to quickly "read" the best route through rocky rapids.

This experience turned out to be very useful once I moved to Arizona. One of my more senior engineers at work, Rolf Andresen, ran, on the side, a white water rafting business together with his three sons. Having heard many of my stories about canoeing back east, Rolf invited me to join him, his family, and friends on a white water rafting trip down the Middle Fork of the Salmon River in Idaho. With more than a little trepidation, I signed on to join him – provided that I could go in whichever boat that he goes in. And, of course, I volunteered to help with whatever chores that I was assigned. The Middle Fork of the Salmon River is in the middle of the River of No Return Wilderness Area in central Idaho. Now, isn't that name ominous enough?

Mid-July 1985 I found myself at the launch site of the Salmon River's Middle Fork together with four inflatable oar rafts, two paddle rafts – all

22+ ft. long – and one 13 ft. paddle raft. These were to carry twenty two of us, including my son Scott, for a week down the river. (An "oar raft" is a rubber, inflatable raft with one captain who maneuvers his boat with a single pair of oars while everyone else on the boat just holds on and tries to keep from falling out. In a "paddle raft" everyone has his own paddle and uses it according to the instructions from the paddler assigned to be the captain.)

Rolf chose to start out in the right rear position in his 13 ft. German-built Metzler paddle raft and instructed me to take the left rear position. I was pleased. And we were soon launched. As we rounded the first river bend, we faced a slew of angry-looking rapids. This would be our first trial. Rolf took a look at the rapids and immediately asked me what route I'd recommend we use to get through them. Well, advice is free, so I stared ahead for half a minute and recommended a route to Rolf. He followed that route and it worked, and we were soon through them and facing the next set of rapids. Once more he asked for my advice, and, once more, used the route that I had suggested. And we were successful. And that's the way that the entire morning went. Of course, I assumed that he was following my recommended routes each time simply because it matched the route that he could also see – and would have used anyway – so I didn't think anything of it.

But, after our lunch break, Rolf got on one of his boy's raft and announced, to my shock and dismay, that I had passed his "test" and that from now on I was in charge of "my" raft. He said that in every case I had selected a good route through the various rapids and, often, better than the route that he would have chosen. OK, now that I was fully in charge, I was as nervous as a wet hen. It's one thing for me to make a route recommendation to Rolf, who could accept or reject it, but now it's all my responsibility and I needed to be especially cautious.

And that concern was not ill placed because, by the time we made camp that evening, only 7 miles into our 100 mile trip, we had managed to get holes punched in the flotation tubes of two of the rafts, several boats suffered holes in the raft floor, and two oars were broken – this due, at least in part, to the water level being much lower than expected making successfully negotiating the rapids more difficult. One boat was completely abandoned with all of its gear and people spread among the other six boats. "My" boat survived intact.

The next three days went much better for the rafters with no new boat damage. We had instead wonderful wilderness scenery to study from our river view, lots of hot springs that all had to be checked out, and excellent fishing. (The river was zoned for "catch-and-release" fishing only, but what can you do if a fish accidentally falls into a heated frying pan at dinner time?)

Disaster struck again on Day 5 when one of the rafts suffered a 2 ½ ft. long cut in one side air chamber while going through Tappan Rapids, an especially challenging set of rapids that was really a small waterfall. We had to first figure out how to sew up this cut to regain structural integrity before trying to make it airtight again. That took some time, but we eventually succeeded.

That evening we were joined by two US Forest Service "River Rangers" in kayaks. Their job all summer long was to kayak this river every week from start to finish to keep an eye on camp site cleanliness and to assist with any emergencies. What a wonderful summer job that would be. We sure envied their opportunity. I think they elected to stay with us for the remaining three days because several of our raft passengers were especially easy to look at – and we fed them well! We ended our trip on Day 7 right at Mile Post 100 as our river merged with the main Salmon River. We all agreed that this Middle Fork Valley had been as beautiful a wilderness area as any of us had ever seen before, but that it had also been far more of a navigational challenge, too, than any of us had ever experienced.

Colorado River in the Grand Canyon

In the sport of white water rafting, one of the classic trips to run is the Colorado River through the Grand Canyon. While there are some rivers bigger than the Colorado River, and certainly many that are more technically challenging than the Colorado River, none combine the volume, difficulty, and scenic and historic beauty like the Colorado River through the Grand Canyon. Many people who've never been in a raft in white water have heard of the river's famous Crystal Rapids and Lava Falls. Commercial river rafting companies are often booked years in advance and the lottery basis for securing a permit to run a private trip can often take twenty years to get drawn. But my good friend Rolf Andresen found a "hole" in the private permit system and took advantage of it to get us a permit for a river trip only three months out.

I got invited to join him on this planned two week long rafting adventure – provided that I agreed to accept his assignment for me. That assignment was to, once again, captain his little thirteen foot four-person Metzler paddle raft and be the group's navigator. I immediately accepted thinking that this would be a very easy assignment. What could be hard about navigating on a river? Pick out the smallest passenger, toss him in the river in the morning, and see which direction he floats. That's downstream! What else is there to know? But Rolf explained that with my little, but very maneuverable raft, my job would be to locate all of the many sights along the way that were worth exploring, and to get to shore in time to signal all of the other rafts where to land since the longer rafts were much less maneuverable than mine. That also meant that I had to keep careful track of precisely where we were at every moment lest a major rapid sneak up on us unprepared. Of course, that also meant that I had to go first! That certainly put a different slant on my assignment. I would be leading the others down a river that I had never seen before. And with my tiny raft, compared with the other 22 foot rafts, I had good reason to be nervous.

And so it was in March 1986, one year after our rafting trip down the Middle Fork of the Salmon River in Idaho, we found ourselves at Lee's

Ferry, river permit in hand, just a dozen miles downstream from the Glen Canyon Dam, ready to launch. But first we had to suffer inspection by a Park Service ranger. Their requirements filled four pages of "must have" stuff, like regulation life jackets for all passengers, proper latrine equipment, aerial signaling devices, and fire pans, etc., etc., etc. But, interestingly, the Park Service places no requirements on the boats to be used. With your permit in hand, you could run the river in a bathtub if you so choose – so long as you had all of the required safety equipment on board.

Our park ranger advised us that at the current water flow rate of 36,000 cubic feet per second, most experienced boaters would not want to run the river with anything less than a 25 foot raft and our rafts were only around 23 feet long. That's when I realized that the ranger had not even noticed my little 13 foot raft since it sat in the shadow of one of the larger rafts. I started to sweat! My raft might be a little on the light side to say the least. Oh well; I wasn't ready to back out now, but I sure knew that my job in the really big rapids was to somehow avoid the really big rapids!

We departed with fifteen people spread across four boats: three oar boats and my little paddle raft. (An oar boat has a single captain manning a pair of oars while each passenger's job was to hold on and not fall out – while my paddle raft had a crewman, with a paddle, on each of the four corners, operating under the instructions of the paddler designated as the captain.)

Fortunately for me, the Colorado River in the Grand Canyon is very well mapped, on water-resistant paper, with all of the rapids marked and rated, and all note-worthy features called out. That helped my navigation assignment a lot.

The Colorado River in the Grand Canyon also has its own rating system with the smallest riffle rated as a '1,' and the biggest rapids, like Lava Falls and Crystal Rapids earning a '10' rating.

We launched at noon – in 44° F water under sunny skies – floating downstream at about 4 – 6 miles per hour. The rapids started right away and so my crew got lots of training in those first couple hours. We were soon a polished team. Soaking wet and cold, but polished none the less - in lots of Class 5, 6, and 7 rapids. We made 18 miles on the water that first afternoon.

On Day 2 we covered almost 20 miles of continuous Class 5 rapids – with lunch in South Canyon where we explored ancient Anasazi ruins, Stanton's Cave, and a beautiful ivy-covered shoreline called Vasey's Paradise.

On Day 3 we realized that the Park Service must have assigned us our very own personal black raven because he stayed right with us as we boated down the river. At first it was sort of cute, but he quickly became a real pest stealing our gorp, chocolate bars, and soap. It even flew off with some of our Brillo pads that had been lying out to dry following dinner clean up.

Several crew members took their turn piloting the oar boats and in the process three of them ended up getting flipped completely out of their boat into the water – and, in one case, breaking an oar in the process. I guess the oar boat captain's job wasn't as easy as it looked. We did get to explore an ancient Anasazi granary during lunch at Nankoweap Canyon.

On Day 4 we passed the confluence with the Little Colorado River, which, due to recent rains, was very muddy – and it muddied the main Colorado River for the rest of the way down the river. One more crew member tried his hand at oaring his raft through Class 8 Hance Rapids and ended up in the drink – losing an oar in the process. Another crew member met a similar fate in Class 9 Sockdolager Rapids – this all in water that had only warmed up to a temperature of 46° F.

On Day 5 we reached the famous Phantom Ranch at the lower end of the South Rim trails where we restocked our fresh water supply. We overnighted a short distance downstream at the Hermit Creek Campsite where five of our crew hiked up to the South Rim and went home – replaced by six others who hiked down from the top on that same trail to join us. We were almost 100 miles into our 200 mile float trip.

I started off on Day 6 with a new crew who had to learn their jobs quickly because the Hermit Rapids, a major Class 10 rapids, began almost immediately out of camp. We did portage around a 100 yard section at the top of Class 10 Crystal Rapids a little later, but ran everything else that day successfully.

Day 7, Easter, had us in very heavy water all day long, but we did stop to visit beautiful Elves Chasm before camping at Tapeats Creek. Because the main river was still very muddy, the fish had all entered the side streams to feed, and so our fishing efforts there were well rewarded. We had trout for dinner that night. While we were running around in shorts, we could easily see fresh snow high on the canyon rim. The river water temperature had only climbed up to 49° F – still a little chilly for end-of-the-day bathing, so I was still delighted to have along my hot solar shower kit to use each evening.

We took the next day off, Day 8, to hike up to the spectacular falls at the head of Thunder River, played horseshoes, and got in more fishing and resting.

On Day 9 we planned our day to camp as close as practical to the Havasu Creek outlet with a hope of stopping there the following morning and hiking up to the popular and scenic Mooney and Havasu Falls. But it didn't quite work out. On Day 10, while I was able to get my raft to shore at the creek outlet and signal its exact location to the other boats, with the high water volume, they were not able to successfully dock there and we had to miss that opportunity.

Day 11 was, for many of us, our most challenging day yet. We had to negotiate the notorious Lava Falls. The larger boats could successfully negotiate these rapids if they could manage to stay centered in the main flow with their bow forward – which they all managed to do – though many of them got the ride of their lives. My only hope in my little boat was to miss the main flow in order to avoid getting flipped end-for-end. I did manage to negotiate a path that avoided that main flow, but a critical captain's error had us drop into a deep whirlpool-like sink hole dumping all of us unceremoniously into the cold water. We all managed to recover from that disaster with nothing lost but our pride, but I had to eat crow for the rest of the trip.

Day 12, our last full day on the river, was uneventful – at least up until one of my crewmates fell out of the raft while negotiating the "mere" Class 7 Kolb Rapids. He was quickly rescued and we proceeded to what would be our final campsite, because the next morning, after a short five more miles, we would be at our trip's end at Diamond Creek, 225 miles downriver from our start at Lee's Ferry.

Postscript 1: The disappointment at not getting to visit Mooney and Havasu Falls was not without at least some serendipity. One young lady in our group - on her first ever in her life camping trip – was not having fun and was secretly planning on bailing out of our trip at Havasu Creek. She was thinking that she could, somehow, hike up and out of the canyon there and find a way to get back home – swearing to never try this sort of thing again. (Rolf and I knew that if she did attempt to hike out, we'd have to assign someone to hike out with her lest she get lost along the way.)   I mention this here because by the end of our trip she did come to love what we were doing and was actually crying when the trip was finally over - wishing that it could continue for another week or two! Talk about a mid-trip transformation!

Postscript 2: Using his "secret" technique, Rolf was able to snag another permit to run the Colorado River in the Grand Canyon in May 1988. I was, once more, invited to join his team – in the same role as for the 1986 trip. And I gladly accepted. The water level was significantly lower than for the 1986 trip: 11,000 cubic feet/second (cfs) versus the 1986 level of 36,000 cfs. As a result we had fewer "disasters" in the rapids, though we did have one raft flip over in House Rock Rapids. That year the Little Colorado River was running a striking aqua-marine blue – which colored the main river blue for some distance down river.   And we did manage this time to stop at Havasu Creek long enough for some of us to hike upstream to Mooney Falls – a truly memorable experience.

Rio Usumacinta

In March 1989, one year after our second rafting trip down through the Grand Canyon, our white water rafting team became aware of an exotic rafting opportunity down a section of the Rio Usumacinta. Along with revealing some ancient Mayan ruins along the way, this river serves as the international border between the state of Chiapas, Mexico, and Guatemala. Rafting it would truly be an exotic international experience – especially since Guatemala was in the middle of a civil war with much of the rebel activity occurring nearby this river.

While they could, I suppose, have contracted to join a regular commercial trip down the river, this team opted to truck three of their own rafts down to Chiapas in order to run their own trip there. And because they pretty much had no idea what they were getting themselves into, they managed to lure Scott Davis, originally from Tucson, into being their guide. Scott had run any number of commercial raft tours down this river, so they had his experience to draw on.

The team brought together to participate in this trip were recruited from the crews of our earlier rafting trips in Arizona and Idaho. Son Scott and I signed on to join them – bringing the crew count to fourteen – plus our guide.

Except for the two driving the supply truck down from Tucson, the rest of us flew to Villahermosa, via Mexico City, where we made our way to the famous Mayan ruins of Palenque before joining up with our boats at the river. The Palenque ruins gave us our first taste of Mayan architecture and their accompanying glyphs depicting their calendar, rulers, and other features of these ancient peoples. In addition to paddling through a truly tropical forest, along with all of its resident wildlife, seeing more Mayan ruins in various stages of recovery from the forest was a principal driver for this trip.

Once in Chiapas, four of us were assigned to pick up food for our trip, arrange for our truck to get parked at our expected river take-out location, and return to our river put-in spot. This would normally have been very quick except that our local Mexican shuttle vehicle got stuck in the sand once and broke down four times on the way, requiring repair by fading flashlight in the middle of the night. Welcome to Mexico!

We started loading our three boats shortly after sunrise that next morning and we were ready to launch by – 2:00 PM! Fortunately, we didn't have far to go that first day – making camp on the Mexican side only a dozen or so miles downstream. I was in charge of one 16 ft. paddle boat, together with a co-captain, with the crew spread between my boat and our second boat, a 16 ft. oar boat – with all of our heavy gear loaded into a third special large oar boat.

We camped for that first night on a sandy shore on the Mexican side of the river, just a short walk from the famous Mayan ruins called Yaxchilan, which loosely translated from Mayan means "green rocks" – named for these moss-covered ruins.

That next morning the attendant caretaker gave us a complete tour of these ruins and their role in the ancient Mayan culture. Of course, his lecture was all in Spanish, but we had plenty of translators in our crew. An important part of his discussion was that these ruins had not been recovered from the jungle all that long ago. At present they were accessible only by the river, but he hoped to one day have access by road – opening up the ruins to more tourists. We continued down the river that afternoon – only occasionally having to deal with the river's infrequent and lame rapids.

Much of the first half of our trip was in largely uninhabited and unexplored rain forest wilderness with much of the second half turned into new settlements, refugee camps, oil exploration sites, and plans for future hydroelectric projects.

At 5 PM we tried landing at a beautiful campsite on the Guatemalan side only to be chased off by armed Guatemalan guerrillas. (We think that they were expecting some sort of secret "delivery" there that night and didn't want any witnesses.) So, reluctantly, we continued downriver - through a narrow, steep-walled canyon, in the setting sun - until we found an acceptable campsite right at dark – this one also on the Guatemalan side. There we saw lots of foot prints on its sandy beach, but had no more guerrillas to deal with that night.

Our concern with these guerrilla contacts, as infrequent as they turned out to be, was twofold. First, the obvious disparity in income between us and these peasants was huge and made us an easy and attractive target for money. And, since our government was supporting their government and not the rebel cause, they could hold that against us. But, in fact, the guerrillas that we encountered throughout our trip felt that we "commoners" had about as much control over our government as they had over theirs, and so they wouldn't hold that against us. We were careful to share some of our stored food with them at every encounter.

That following day we made one stop to hike to a beautiful lake on the Mexican side – spying the bones of two caiman along the way. All along we were seeing and hearing beautiful toucans, spider monkeys, and howler monkeys in the jungle on both sides of the river – often very noisy all night long.

The following day had us continuing down river, through even more rain forest, watching for all sorts of critters – two-legged as well as four-legged.

Near lunchtime, with help from guide Scott, we selected a spot on the beach on the Guatemalan side for lunch - adjacent to a faint trail. This trail eventually led us to the old Mayan ruins called Piedras Negra, or "Black Rocks." What was unique here was that these ruins were still totally overgrown by the surrounding jungle and so it was hard to assess their full extent. There was some evidence that fortune hunters had already disturbed much of the ruins looking for treasures, but it wouldn't be until sometime in the future when the government could afford the effort required to clear these ruins from the jungle and make them available for tourist viewing.

I was a bit on edge examining these ruins because guide Scott had warned us to be on the lookout for a special green vine snake that was especially poisonous - and I had already almost stepped on one! A short while later a second one was spotted.

We also discovered that we were, once again, only a few hundred yards from another guerrilla training camp. We high-tailed it out of there shortly after they paid us a visit!

We found another perfect sandy beach campsite later that afternoon albeit once again on the Guatemalan side. And while we didn't see or hear any more rebel soldiers, the sand around our campsite that next morning was totally covered with heavy boot tracks! A quick inventory showed nothing missing though, and so we once more launched the boats and breathed a sigh of relief.

Over the next couple days, as we drifted down river, we passed any number of small Indian villages and coffee plantations – all on the Mexican side of the river. The peoples on these villages were all friendly and delighted to see folks from the "outside" though our communication with them was limited since almost none of them spoke Spanish or English, but only a version of Mayan.

After finishing up our trip in Tenosique and returning to our starting point, we took a day off to relax and then went on a long, one-day raft trip down the nearby Rio Shumulja. We were watching particularly for its intersection with the Rio Xanil – which was the outflow from the spectacular Agua Azul waterfalls – a series of over a half dozen sensational aquamarine blue waterfalls. Some of us hiked up to view and photograph the first six waterfalls – each cascading into its own limestone travertine pool – before continuing on to the next falls.

What a natural and culturally rich and stimulating trip this turned out to be for all of us.

Chapter Six

Cycling

Tibet

A few years before I retired, I ran across a brochure from REI, put out by their adventure travel branch, describing their month long Asian mountain bike adventure from Lhasa, the capital of Tibet, to Kathmandu, the capital of Nepal, with a planned side trip to the north side base camp of Mt. Everest. Since the Himalaya defines the international border between Tibet and Nepal, this can only mean that this cycling adventure crosses the famous Himalaya. There is a rough, but passable dirt/gravel road the whole way - in various stages of dis-repair - that was put in many years ago, called the Friendship Highway, which connects Lhasa with Kathmandu. What an exciting adventure that would make. I made myself a promise to look into this trip just as soon as I retired and was able to see my way clear to taking a month-long mountain bike travel adventure.

You can imagine, then, my disappointment when, upon retiring, REI responded to my inquiry saying that they no longer ran that trip. I was devastated. But a short while later I discovered that KE Adventures, a travel adventure company out of England, was operating just such a trip. With obvious excitement I immediately signed up with them. And in September Y2000 I was on a flight to Kathmandu, via Tokyo and Bangkok, with my old mountain bike safely disassembled and boxed up. I was so worried that somehow I would get separated from my bike that at the airport in Bangkok, where I had an overnight stop, I had the airline personnel verify that my bike made it onto our 45 minute flight to Kathmandu.

Despite this effort though, my bike box mysteriously disappeared in the

Kathmandu Airport's luggage claim area. And, curiously, even before I could round up an official to report the loss, I had a local citizen tap me on the shoulder to offer me a deal on a rental bike for a month. What a scam! But I was helpless. Fuming, I contracted for one of his rental bikes: a Scott Model 7005 aluminum bike with 8 speed Shimano SIS gearing and front suspension. At least it was a decent bike for the task ahead.

I then met up with our group consisting of fourteen cyclists – split evenly between Brits and Yankees and also split evenly between guys and gals – plus a British guide, Karl, and a Nepali bike mechanic/team boss/rider, Rashesh.

We flew together that very next day, on a one hour flight, to Lhasa, Tibet. Lhasa is at the surprisingly high elevation of around 14,000 ft. We spent the next four days cycling and touring around Lhasa while we got acclimatized to the elevation before leaving town. We toured the famous Barkor Square, the Jokhang Temple, and the popular Potala where the current Dalai Lama would reside if he hadn't left Tibet years ago fearing for his life from the over-powering Chinese government. On our third day there Karl was notified that my "lost" bike has suddenly reappeared in Kathmandu. That was sure of mixed comfort. It wouldn't do me any good now, but at least I should have a bike to take back home at the end of our tour.

After four full days in Lhasa we decided that we were sufficiently acclimatized and started off on our journey up and over the Himalaya. Our first day out of town was about 55 miles long, and no one seemed to have any trouble with that. But the second day was a different story as our route had us climbing a 6% grade for fourteen miles. Many were already suffering headaches from the altitude though only two opted for a lift to camp.

Our support team consisted of four Toyota Land Cruisers and two Chinese Army trucks, all with Tibetan drivers, to haul our duffels, tents, and kitchen supplies. The kitchen staff consisted of two chief cooks, and 4 – 5 helpers, all Nepali Sherpa. They served us three hot meals every day.

The next day took an even higher toll. It turned out that Trevor, one of the Brits, and I were the only ones to cycle to the top of that day's pass,

Koro La. All of the others took a lift at one point or another. We started out the day in freezing temps and after negotiating a very wet crossing, which got my legs and feet soaked, I was freezing, too. Oh well; welcome to the mountainous Tibetan Himalaya. There was not a lot of wildlife to be seen, but there were plenty of horses, cows, sheep, goats, and yaks.

Once in camp, Karl shuttled two down to Gyanste, where we were headed that next day, so that hopefully they might recover faster from their altitude issues. Karl and Rashesh both bent the rim on one of their bike's wheels with their fast descent off the pass and so they spent much of the evening straightening them enough to make them rideable again.

As expected, that next day was an easy 50 km downhill and level ride to Gyantse where we stayed in a real hotel – which meant real showers. We were riding at about half strength today as a result of both altitude headaches and stomach problems. I had my first exposure to Chinese Pabst Blue Ribbon beer and boiled chicken feet. One out of the two wasn't bad!

The following day we were riding back at full strength as we toiled on to the city of Shigatse on a long, flat, dusty, bumpy road for about 95 km (about 60 miles), another hotel stay, another hot shower, and then were rewarded with a day off. Shigatse's claim to fame was that it is the home of the famous and striking Tashithumpo Monastery – built especially for the Panchen Lama – the second in command to the Dalai Lama. The Panchen Lama's chief task in life is to choose the new Dalai Lama when the old one dies. And so the Chinese authorities have taken a special interest in the current Panchen Lama – schooling him exclusively in Beijing – so that he'd, hopefully, bend to the Chinese leader's preferences when it came time to exercise his duty. The monastery housed a statue of Buddha – thought to be the world's largest indoor Buddha at 60 ft. in height.

After our day of rest, we tackled our longest day yet – 105 km (about 63 miles) – against a stiff headwind. Only six of us cycled the whole way that day. Soon followed a climb the next day to Tso La at 4,500 m. (14,760 ft.) elevation – followed soon after that by the Gyatso La at 5250 m. (17,220 ft.) elevation in a light snow storm. OK, now it's starting to get serious! When you are cycling uphill at these elevations, you are not focused on reaching the top, but rather on just reaching the next kilometer marker for a two minute break off the bike. I quickly realized that to take a drink of water required stopping the bike, because I could not afford the loss of one single breath while swallowing and still pedal! And eating an energy bar required finding a spot to sit down to save energy.

On one occasion, while pedaling uphill, I recall having passed kilometer marker number 4470, and so, after a short break, I continued uphill looking for KM 4471. After what seemed like forever, I convinced myself that the KM 4471 marker had slid off the mountain somewhere and was lost, and so I began watching for the KM 4472 marker. But once again, after what seemed like forever, I convinced myself that it, too, was missing in action, and began watching for KM 4473. Shortly thereafter I spied, off in the far distance, a KM marker. That heartened me to dig in and reach it – only to discover – of course – that it was KM 4471! What a disappointment. To say the least, climbing was very slow at those elevations.

That evening we were joined in camp by Shane, a young boy from Gunnison, Colorado, who was cycling around the world. He had started over two years earlier in Alaska, cycled south to Chile, on to New Zealand and Australia, through south east Asia, and was now headed for Kathmandu. We quit complaining about that day's climb once we realized that he had climbed it, too, on a bike loaded with all of his travel gear.

Karl opened our "medical clinic" that evening and set out the "Doctor Is In" sign: We had one dental cap that had to be glued back in place and a cut knee that needed to be sewn up. I was told that we were approximately half way to Kathmandu.

Two days later, after topping out at Pang La, we finally got our first view of Mt. Everest. And it wasn't all that far away. We could also see Lhotse, Makalu, Pumori, and Cho Oyo - all 8,000 meter Himalayan cousins of Mt. Everest. That was really exciting for me. Coming down off that pass, we soon found ourselves riding toward a side road that led to the old town of Rongbuk at 4,920 m. (16,137 ft.) elevation. It held special meaning to me because that is where the Rongbuk Monastery would be that marked the base camp for George Mallory, and his British team, when he made the very first attempts to climb Mt. Everest in the early 1920's. We, too, set up our camp there for a couple days – in full view of the north side of Mt. Everest. (Mallory and his climbing partner, Sandy Irvine, died very high on Everest on their summit attempt in 1923.) Air temperatures were in the 40's there at base camp, though it felt like 80 in the bright sun. We had a perfect view of Mt. Everest from this side silhouetted by a bright, clear blue sky – without a storm in sight. We were surprised to not find evidence of any climbing parties on this side of the mountain since we were at the very height of the fall climbing season.

That next morning, our declared "rest day," we awoke to a temperature of 22° F. Shortly after breakfast we all went for a hike up the Mt. Everest trail. I was in my glory. As time went by various folks decided that they had had all of this fun that they needed and turned back – eventually reducing our hiking group size to just Karl and me. And we, too, eventually had to stop as a wide chasm opened up in the trail in front of us. So we sat and shared some hot tea and crackers.

When Karl suggested that we turn around here and head back, too, I asked him for our elevation. He told me that we had reached 19,000 ft. elevation – in just a sweater, jeans, and lightweight hiking shoes! That really impressed me, but I didn't let on. Instead, I remarked that if the summit of Everest was around 29,000 ft. and we were already at 19,000 ft., then we only had a "mere" 10,000 ft. – or less than two miles further to go. Surely we could cover two more miles of hiking and still be back in camp in time for lunch, so we should just go on to the summit while the weather was holding. Well, I thought Karl was going to die laughing! He couldn't wait now to get back to camp to tell everyone what I wanted to do. He had fun over that incident for the whole rest of the trip.

That next morning we all got a lift back to the top of Pang La on the main highway where we got back on our bikes and rode to a hot spring – just past the village of Tingri (a town that I would return to many years later for an attempt to climb Cho Oyo). Of course, we all hit the hot spring – for the low price of 10 yuan each. And we stayed there – enjoying the hot water – until the owner came out and dumped the supper dishes in the water with us! That was enough; we quickly got out.

For a time now we had warmer and denser air which really improved our sleep quality at night. Our relatively level terrain continued for another couple days before climbing up to Tong La North at almost 17,000 ft. elevation. From there we were able to see Shishapangma, one more of the Himalaya's 8,000 meter peaks (and the only one entirely inside Tibet). We dropped that night to a shallow saddle at about 16,100 ft. elevation from which we had only one more high pass to conquer, Tong La South, at a little over 17,000 ft., before starting our long descent into Nepal.

At dinner that evening Trevor made the mistake of bragging that so far he was the first one to the top of every one of the major passes on our route and he was aiming in the morning to add this last pass to his list. By that point we had cycled over 460 miles on our journey.

That next morning I made a special effort to be fully packed and had my bike ready before breakfast, ate quickly, snuck out of the mess tent, and was soon on my way up to the pass – a 7 km distance. The race was on just as soon as Trevor realized that I had already left. He immediately jumped on his bike and tore off after me. Of course, at 16,000 ft. elevation, neither of us was going very fast, but he was certainly gaining on me with every pedal stroke. I managed to keep up my blistering pace (at what was probably 4 ½ mph!) and did manage to beat him to the pass – stealing this final pass from him. We shook hands and had a good laugh over it, but he was probably steaming inside.

Once the rest of our riders and staff reached this our final pass, we started taking all of the mandatory group shots with both our Nepali and Tibetan support staff – using the majestic Himalaya as our backdrop. Dawa, our head Tibetan driver, in an unusual display of trust, quietly showed me his secret hiding place in his Land Cruiser where he hid his personal photograph of the Dalai Lama. He was very proud of that. I thought that it was interesting that none of us foreigners would have given a second thought to having on our person a photograph of someone that we revered without risk of imprisonment.

Once the cameras were finally put away, we started what would be a continuous 67 km (42 mi.) descent from about 17,000 ft. elevation down to Nyalam at around 12,200 ft. That night in camp at dinner our Tibetan drivers presented us with a case of cold Lhasa beer. Do you think that they knew that we would be reaching the Tibet – Nepal border the next day and this would be their final opportunity to earn an end-of-trip tip?

After an excellent night's sleep at this substantially lower elevation, we continued downhill for another 41 km (25 mi) to Zhang Mu, the international border, and passed through China's immigration control and then rode our bikes across the Friendship Bridge into Nepal – being extra careful to ride halfway across the bridge on the right hand side of the roadway per the standard in Chinese Tibet – switching to the left hand side as we officially entered Nepal and its British driving standard. We spent the night here in Kodari, Nepal, getting our first hot shower in a couple weeks – while our Sherpa staff hand-carried all of our gear and supplies from Zhang Mu to Kodari. We remembered to adjust our clocks and watches back by 2 ¼ hours upon entering Nepal. (All of China operates on Beijing time and Nepali time runs 15 minutes ahead of India time.) By this point we had covered approximately 835 km (520 mi) since leaving Lhasa and our trip was finally grinding to an end.

Shortly after leaving Kodari that next morning, we were on quality tarmac roads. That was a welcome change as we continued downhill into a hot and humid tropical climate. What a contrast from only a few days earlier. We spent our last night camping next to the town of Dhanlukiel (where I was able to buy some cold beer and cookies) on the very rim overlooking Kathmandu – a mere 20 – 25 km away – all downhill!

We were met in the morning by a team of young Nepali mountain bikers who had ridden up from town to our camp to escort us to Kathmandu. Upon arrival at our hotel in town we had logged a total of 950 km (590 mi.) over this past month. That night it was our turn to treat our staff; we took them all out to dinner at a nearby Indian restaurant.

Our overall trip schedule had included a couple "rain days," which we never needed, and so we used those days in Kathmandu and the surrounding Thamel Valley to explore a variety of Hindu and Buddhist temples – some dating back more than 2,000 years. An afternoon spent repacking all of our bikes had us ready for the long flights home. I still hadn't seen my "recovered" bike, but on the way to the airport that next morning, we stopped at a very nondescript building and, lo and behold, back in the corner was my bike box – with everything intact. I never did learn anything more about its path to that building, but was still glad to have it returned. And, many months later, I got a reimbursement check, without explanation, from Thai Airlines for my trouble.

The Pig & I

Or, How I Came To Stop Hating the Pig and Start Loving the BOB

There I was, late in the hot afternoon, still dragging "the pig," and heading up a very long and steep mountain grade, with cars and giant trucks whizzing by inches away, after having already ridden well over 90 miles for the day, and wondering, "Whatever was I thinking when I signed on to this foolhardy fiasco?" Off in the distance behind me were my two equally stalwart but equally drained companions, Smilin' Steve Wilson and Devilish Donna Lewandowski. As it would happen, when we eventually joined up on top of the windy climb, they, too, were wondering on the merits of our carefully laid travel plan.

We were climbing 6,000 feet to the first of six summits crossing the San Bernardino Mountains on Interstate 8 in southern California – within sight of the Mexican border – and were totally exhausted. We had just climbed the equivalent of a ride up Tucson's Mt. Lemmon, fully loaded. By the time we reached that first summit we had ridden a total of over 400 miles and this was only the fourth day of our scheduled six-day journey. Was this really four centuries back-to-back? We didn't want to think about it. We only wanted to eat and sleep. And to make matters worse, I had just discovered a pig inside my "pig."

Devilish Donna admitted to having dreamed up this crazy idea some six months earlier, but it took her that long to get the courage to even propose it. She had long dreamed of wanting to cycle, fully self-contained, from Tucson to her folk's home in Tustin, California – near Los Angeles. And she picked the university's March spring break week in which to do it. Once the laughter died down and Smilin' Steve saw that she was serious, he knew that somehow he would have to figure out how to pull this off or he would never hear the end of it.

Early in the planning stage in the spring of 2002 he called me with an outline of their plan and I told him that trying to ride almost 600 miles in six days, against prevailing March winds, was ludicrous. But I had also revealed that I had already dragged out the maps before announcing my view, and Smilin' Steve knew right then and there that I was hooked. I just couldn't let those two ride off and do this trip and be bragging about it for the next year without me along. I would have always been wondering if I were tough enough to have done it, too.

Unfortunately, I had not only never ridden anyplace self-contained before, I didn't even own a bike that I could use for such a trip. This obstacle was soon solved when a good friend offered me a BOB ("Beast of Burden") trailer that he had used on a recent six month trip to New Zealand. The BOB is a one-wheeled, low profile contraption that attaches to the bike's rear axle quick release mechanism thus placing virtually no stress on the bike's frame itself. Now I could use one of my racing-style bikes with nothing left to buy. Yes, now I was really committed since I no longer had a good excuse to back out. My training, too, now picked up in earnest. I actually got on my bike – something I'd not done in several months! Did I think this trip would be easy?

My first re-awakening came a week before the trip when I actually picked up the BOB trailer and tried it out. The first trip around the neighborhood, empty of course, was actually fun. Tying on a simulated load of 25 pounds was a horse of a different color. Now the bike-trailer assembly became very unstable. It was even difficult getting the whole business upright to start with. And attempting to stand to pedal was totally out of the question. The natural swaying of the bike produced a like swaying of the trailer – which fed quickly back to the bike and soon the whole mess was headed for a pre-mature crash and burn. And pulling this whole load was something like dragging a dead pig on a short leash. It had a stubborn mind of its own and quickly came to be referred to as "the pig" at every opportunity. I really didn't like this whole business and I was way out of my comfort zone. I wished for a tactful way to back out of this commitment.

I did discover that lighter loads were somewhat easier to handle and so I started a crash effort to carve off unnecessary weight. I reduced my tire tool count from the usual three tools to two, extracted the stuff sacks from my tent and Thermarest air mattress, and opted for one less spare tube. That reduced the overall load by 8 ounces, a whopping 1%! I knew I was in trouble then. I did manage to remove a few clothing items, but for everything that came off, another "necessary" last minute item took its place. I continued to worry.

And to add to my pile of worry beads was food. Though we committed up front to take all of our meals in restaurants and overnights in motels, we also knew that these didn't come in convenient 100 mile intervals. And so, in addition to tents and sleeping bags, we had to be prepared to travel equipped with food and kitchen supplies. I was tickled when Devilish Donna announced that she would take care of any dinner food requirements. In my haste I had forgotten that she was a vegan! That oversight eventually came to plague me.

Our trip officially started with Smilin' Steve and Devilish Donna, on their equally over loaded tandem, at 7:00 AM from their driveway at the base of Mt. Lemmon. Their loaded bike weighed in at well over 100 pounds. And our first stop was for breakfast on Fourth Avenue, near downtown, with several friends who had, for a good laugh, cycled that far with us. Do you know how many incredibly long and steep grades there are between the city's northeast side and Fourth Avenue? I thought I'd remembered having climbed Mt. Lemmon itself with less effort.

Lunch, many miles and hours later, was near the Kitt Peak turn-off on the Ajo Highway – barely out of sight of the city. And by dusk we were at Quijotoa, a tiny Indian trading post 22 miles west of Sells. Our planned water stop here was a near disaster when we discovered that the trading post had closed early and none of its outside faucets were working. Devilish Donna saved the day by scaring up the needed liquid in the middle of a nearby construction project and we were soon cooking dinner nestled in a tiny roadside wash just as the sun was setting in the west. Coyotes lulled us to sleep in our tents as we reveled in our first 100 mile day.

The second day on the road took us on to the town of Why and then to Ajo, Arizona, for lunch and north to Gila Bend for dinner. Smilin' Steve remarked, as we were leaving Ajo, that we had been riding now for some fifteen hours total and weren't even out of Pima County! By this time I had already had several long talks with "the pig" and we were starting to reach a better understanding. But I still didn't have any luck pedaling while standing and was starting to get concerned about how I would get up the serious grades ahead with little more than racing gears on the bike. Maybe I should have taken my mountain bike after all.

With a little over an hour to sunset and most of our journey still in front of us, we left Gila Bend, following dinner, and headed west on I-8 to hunt up a usable campsite. We eventually stopped at a vacant field, right beside the Union Pacific rail line, just as the sun disappeared. And we were quickly in our sleeping bags under a glorious sky, lulled to distraction by the frequent train whistles, after now having completed our second century.

Day three's challenge was now obvious to us. If we could make Yuma by nightfall, we could look forward to hot showers, clean riding shorts, and real beds – and just maybe a hot tub for good measure. Fortunately, we again had favorable winds and got to Yuma with the last light - another 100 mile day. We mused over just how much more riding we would have risked in the dark if it had taken us any longer.

Our fourth day, with the dreaded climbs up into the San Bernardino Mountains still in front of us, started in the cool morning air crossing the lazy Colorado River into California. The trip through the sand dune country was magical with the occasional wildflower on display, but the fatigue of the previous three days was starting to take its toll. The first casualty was our intent to use frontage and other side roads whenever they were available. This is, in fact, a requirement of California freeway cycling. As Smilin' Steve characterized it, before using the freeway shoulder for riding, even 20 year old goat paths must first be exhausted. But the I-8 shoulders were enticing; they were consistently wide, clean, straight, and smooth. And we almost made it to Ocotillo at the base of the mountains before getting chased – and chastised – by the local CHP's squad. One more exit and we'd have it made, but it was not to be. Our choice side road here took us to and through famous Plaster City – followed by mile after unending mile of very bumpy, unused, hot, sticky, miserable, sweaty, boring roadway before again rejoining the freeway. We cursed the CHP's officer all the while and that made us feel better. On the positive side, since my butt was already on strike with the seat, I got a lot more practice standing up while pedaling and pulling the "pig" and finally felt that I had mastered it. I was ready to be tested on a decent grade and that grade was now right in front of us.

Once at the top of that seemingly endless grade, we were more than ready to get off the bikes, more than ready to devour a bunch of real food, and more than ready to hit the hay. Unfortunately, while we did snag a good place to camp for the night, we did not snag any real food! Instead, Devilish Donna had planned our campsite meal for the night. And because she was a dyed-in-the-wool vegan, we weren't going to eat any "real" food, but instead we'd be eating grass, leaves, and twigs, or whatever it is that vegan's eat. Actually, what she prepared, though unrecognizable, was very tasty. However, after our long, strenuous ride that day, I needed a bucket full and not a bowl full. I licked the pot clean and was still hungry enough to eat the pot, too! Needless to say, I turned in still starving.

Right before I dozed off I remembered that I had packed away a very large piece of homemade spice cake – brought along just for this kind of occasion – easily enough for three people. I dug it out of my duffel, unwrapped it, and quickly divided it into three pieces. While I devoured one of the three pieces I observed that my two hardy companions had already turned in, too, and seemed to already be sound asleep. Then it occurred to me that Devilish Donna probably wouldn't be able to eat her share of the cake anyway because it wasn't vegan. So, I ate her piece, too, and fell fast asleep. When I had occasion to get up in the middle of that starry night, I looked long and hard at the third piece of cake. It looked awfully lonely. So I ate it, too, and never mentioned it again.

Our night out on top of that San Bernardino Mountain pass was quite eventful – or so I was told the next morning. I slept through it all. Supposedly there were trucks circling our little encampment in the wee hours and migrants from across the nearby border hiding around our camp. Or did Devilish Donna just dream it? In any case, while unpacking that night I discovered that a small, ceramic pig had found its way into my duffel. That provided no end of comic relief for us. And that came to be how there was "a pig in my pig!"

Breakfast that next morning was going to be at the very first restaurant that we saw - in whatever was the very next town that we came to. None the less, I couldn't make it there without stopping to dig into my duffel for an English muffin and some peanut butter just to tide me over until then.

Not unlike Day #3, our fifth day presented us with another obvious challenge. If we could make it to San Diego before dark, we could once more look forward to hot showers and real beds. The problem was that our engines were starting to get cranky and we had yet to complete the crossing of the San Bernardino Mountains in what was now a very stiff headwind that never left us. After breakfast in Jacumba, heavy fog in Live Oak Springs, and lunch in Pinedale, we completed the final summit push and started our long descent into San Diego proper.

Now we were on a mission, like horses heading for the barn. Devilish Donna, with the route instructions in one hand and the GPS in the other, pedaling all the while, barked enough instructions to keep us on course and it again became a race with the sun. Into and out of San Diego we went, skirting the Miramar Naval Air Station, and from one bike path to yet another. The sun won the race this time, but with only another 4 – 5 miles to go, we decided to chance it and continued on – finally reaching our destination, Poway, at the top of two desperately steep grades. We were in deep anaerobic debt when we pulled into the driveway of a good friend of Devilish Donna's, but were at the same time elated to have reached our target still alive and still on schedule – now well over 500 miles in five days. Bec, our host, a hauntingly attractive blonde, entertained us with her special house pets, chickens rescued from a local egg ranch, while we showered and recovered. Those beds that night were going to provide us the most comfortable and welcome rest ever.

As a reward to Bec for putting us up for the night, we offered to take her out to any restaurant of her choice. (Of course, we also needed use of her car to get us there.) She thought about it for a minute and asked us if we really meant "any restaurant of her choice?" We were famished and so we repeated our offer. I was already dreaming about a long-awaited steak or lobster – with all of the trimmings. Bec drove us to the restaurant of her choice: Sweet Tomatoes!!! Oh my goodness! More grass, leaves, and twigs! Bec was also a vegan! Just my luck. Fourteen bushels of vegetables later, we tumbled back to her house and died.

That next morning, our final destination now looked achievable. We had less than 85 miles left to ride and were already familiar with the route and the routine. We had only to bid adieu to Bec and her house chickens that next morning, sneak over to the coast, and turn north. We then suffered our first and only breakdown of the trip – a broken rack weld that almost took out the tandem's rear wheel with it. And then, in the middle of the repair, a handful of map sheets flew off into the wind – never to be seen again – since the headwinds that we had picked up the day before were, if anything, gusting even stronger. But there was just no way that we weren't going to finish this trip and later that afternoon, right at dusk, the tandem and the "pig" pulled into Tustin and into Devilish Donna's parent's driveway – ending this epic adventure with a mixture of both well-earned relief and pride.

With all of the introductions that followed, it was announced that we were in for a special treat. Devilish Donna's dad had been practicing all week long on how to make a very unique, all vegan meal for us in celebration of our cycling achievement. When he heard me visibly groan, he quickly agreed to put off that special meal for a day and treat us to a restaurant meal in town that evening. I was elated – until I discovered that it, too, was going to be vegan. I guess if I really wanted meat, I'd have to start chewing on my arm.

Note: A version of this story first appeared in the monthly newsletter of the Greater Arizona Bicycling Association (GABA) in May 2002.

Chapter Seven

Other

U. S. Army

When I entered college as a freshman in 1960 I signed up for ROTC training. With this path I avoided worrying about getting drafted – a near certainty otherwise in my draft district. Upon entering my junior year in college I had to choose to either leave the ROTC program, and be immediately subject to the draft, or commit to serving in the Army following my graduation. And I had two choices there: 1) two years of active duty in the Regular Army, or 2) six months active duty for training in the Regular Army followed by 5 ½ years in the Army Reserve. (The reserve service would have required attending a weekend of training every month plus two weeks of summer camp every summer.)

Obviously, I opted for the latter choice because it would have the least impact on my life (and still keep me out of the war).

This choice appeared to work – until my senior year when the reserve training option suddenly disappeared – without warning – or choice. Welcome to the US Army!

While I did defer this new two year active duty commitment for several years while I was in graduate school, I eventually had to serve it. I entered the service in November 1966.

When that day came, I got orders for what I was assured to be a two year assignment at the Army's Electronic Proving Ground at Fort Huachuca in southern Arizona. Perfect! I got to spend every working day in an air conditioned laboratory, as a test officer, testing and evaluating the Army's latest and greatest communications equipment. Plush! And right up my alley! And that actually worked for the first year. I got to fully test (and reject) a state of the art teletype test generator that was sorely needed by the Army's Signal Corps. It failed completely eight of the ten functional test areas previously agreed to and the design included an electrical hazard that could result in the operator getting electrocuted! Interestingly, the Army decided to field this device anyway, despite my data, since it was so badly needed at the time, and so thousands of them were purchased and distributed – only to end up on the scrap heap months later when they quit working – as I had predicted.

Then I moved on to evaluate a state-of-the-art voice-actuated cryptographic system usable with field radios to provide secure voice communications in the field. I was in my glory!

Soon after that one of the Signal Corps companies stationed at Fort Huachuca received orders to prepare for deployment to Vietnam. It was 1967 – near the peak of the war effort there. The Pentagon immediately started sending GIs fresh out of boot camp and still wet behind the ears to this company in order to bring it up to full combat strength. They came up short! They still needed several more officers to run things in the company. And so the Fort Huachuca base commander was ordered to fill all of the remaining openings with officers from his own command. His adjutant put names in a hat of all of the officers qualified to fill these few remaining slots. And, you guessed it, my name went into the hat and I was one of the "lucky" ones to get selected. Within a week I was in the "real" Army – sharing the command with a half-dozen other officers, none with any combat experience and none with any Signal Corps training either. Though our brand new company commander, a captain, had been in the Army a year or two longer than the rest of us lieutenants, he had no Signal Corps experience at all – having spent his time as some general's driver in Europe somewhere – and also had no command experience either. We were on our own!

Without a clue to what I was doing, I was ordered by this brand new company commander to put together and implement a detailed training plan for the six weeks in front of us that would turn us into a crack communications company ready for a full combat role in Vietnam. What a challenge! I was clueless on how to proceed, but wasn't given any other choice! You do what you have to do!

Our company was what the Army called a totally mobile signal support company designed to provide all of the communications needed between an Army Corps Headquarters, or equivalent, and each of its many divisions and brigades. We were staffed at 348 enlisted men and officers. My official title was Facility Control Officer – responsible for all of the communications capability of our company – but, in practice, it was essentially the second in command of the company, similar to an executive officer in other units.

I rounded up some experienced sergeants and started winging it big time – learning as I went. We spent every one of those weeks in the field, away from base distractions, training night and day. And six weeks later we were ready to go off to war – or as ready as we were going to be. What a steep learning curve!

We did have the full support of everyone at Fort Huachuca, but no one ever told us what to do or how to do it. We were fully on our own. It was overwhelming, but I guess that's how the Army operates. We even had a general fly down from his headquarters at Fort Lewis, Washington, to ask us how much money we'd need to conduct all of this training, but offered no guidance on how to actually make such a calculation. This approach shocked me, but that's the way it was. (They didn't teach me any of that in college ROTC.)

My company commander told me, when this training stage was completed, that he was so impressed with what we had been able to accomplish that once we got to Vietnam he was going to put me in for a Bronze Star, but, of course, with the pressure of war, that never happened.

At the end of our formal field training, I was very busy planning how to get all of our 98 trucks and jeeps, trailers and generators, and other gear packed up and shipped by freight train from Fort Huachuca to Long Beach, California. One step was to figure out precisely how many flat-bed train cars would be needed. My sergeant and I measured the length of our many vehicles, and, knowing the length of train cars, came up with a car count, and placed our order with the Southern Pacific Railroad. Meanwhile we also had the motor pool paint over all of the unit identification on our vehicles as required by the Army. (They didn't teach me any of that in college ROTC, either!)

While this was going on, unbeknownst to me, and as a joke, some members of our company "borrowed" the adjacent company commander's jeep, painted over its identifying insignia, and placed it in the line with the rest of our trucks and jeeps. The affected company commander was livid, of course, and turned out his whole company to scour the entire base looking for his "lost" jeep – to no avail. I was told that that generated considerable hilarity among the officer corps, but I was too busy to appreciate it.

A couple days later our freight train arrived and we began loading up our many vehicles and got them tied down on the train's flat-bed cars. But we came up short. The train cars were full, but we still had one vehicle left over with no place to put it. I got chastised by the commander because I had somehow miscalculated our need – requiring the locomotive engineer to take his engine back to the rail yard to pick up another flat-bed car for our "extra" truck. This cost us a whole day on an already tight schedule. I looked and looked at my calculations, but could not figure out where my error had been. But we were too busy to dwell on this very long and soon we were ready to go.

Once all of our troops were off to Long Beach, California, to catch a ship to Vietnam, along with all of our trucks, trailers, generators, and tons of communication equipment, I joined a team of two other enlisted men from our company who served as a rear party responsible to sign over to the post administration all of our barracks, beds, sheets, blankets, etc. When we inventoried it all before calling for the sign-over, I discovered that we were short hundreds of sheets and blankets and pillows. And I had no idea what to do. But my sergeant wasn't the least bit dismayed by this. He simply "borrowed" the needed items from the adjacent unit's supply room until the turn-over inspection was completed and then returned it. When I questioned him about this process, he said, "Sir, we do this all of the time. It's no big deal!" (They didn't teach me this in college ROTC either.)

Our "rear party" then converted to being an "advance party" as we made arrangements to fly to Vietnam to prepare for our company's arrival in three to four weeks.

And we almost didn't get to go! Since we were going to be flying directly into a combat zone, I didn't see any need for dress uniforms and so I had my small advance party team send their dress uniforms home and plan to fly in our issued combat fatigues. Remember, to that point nobody was ever telling us what to do or how to do it. We were on our own. Well, as we were preparing to take a chartered flight out of Fort Lewis, Washington, directly to Cam Ranh Bay, Vietnam, we were told that U.S. Army policy required dress uniforms in flight. And when I told them that we didn't have any dress uniforms to put on, a lieutenant colonel was rounded up to explain this requirement to us and to announce that we couldn't leave until we were in the proper uniform. Well, I was more than willing to sit in that terminal for an entire year, if necessary, since we didn't have anything else to put on. It would certainly be safer since at least no one would be shooting at us then. But, after a difficult several hours and getting chewed out a couple more times, we boarded our flight and were soon on our way – in combat fatigues.

Once in Vietnam, we were to be temporarily billeted at An Khe, in the Central Highlands, a base shared with the 1st Air Cavalry Division, which was about 50 miles inland from the ship's landing port of Qui Nhon. Our final destination was eventually to be at Phu Bai, a tiny village just south of the ancient city of Hue, north of Da Nang and well up into Northern I Corps, Vietnam. We were to help establish critical communications throughout Northern I Corps from the Pacific Coast west to the Laotian border and north to the DMZ – inter-connecting all of the Army and Marine units there.

While making the many preparations for billeting, food, fuel, ammunition, and the like at An Khe, I got invited (which means ordered) to report to our acting battalion commander at Pleiku near the Laotian border to report on our overall company status.

I hitched a ride there on a helicopter the very next day. I gave the colonel a very detailed description of our company's staffing level, training, and equipment readiness. I made such an impression on this guy with my report that he offered me the command of one of his companies – on the spot! Whoa! That was risky for sure. I sure didn't want a real combat job if I could avoid it. I very tactfully declined his offer saying that I really preferred to stay with my own green company since they, too, needed me. It worked. I returned to An Khe.

In due time my company's transport ship arrived in the harbor of Que Nhon, after having been at sea for a little over three weeks. My sergeant and I drove there to help them get married back up with our company's vehicles and equipment which had also arrived. Once the vehicles were gassed up and the required ammunition issued, we drove to our temporary base at An Kha.

In a curious turn of events, on our first full day at An Khe, one of our GI's had a jeep stolen from him when he stopped at the base commissary to pick up some food supplies. We scoured the entire base looking for it, but it was nowhere to be seen. The company commander was quite upset about this loss since it would look very bad on his record that he lost valuable government property on a secure base. I was not able to console him. As a distraction I asked him to tell me the full story about the company commander's jeep loss at Fort Huachuca when we were there. He delighted in telling me how they had pulled off this joke on that captain. But when I asked him how they managed the return of his jeep following that incident, he said that he didn't really know, but that he was sure that "someone" took care of that. All of a sudden a light went off in my head. Just maybe my problem with having one too many vehicles to load onto the train at Fort Huachuca involved this extra jeep. And so that next morning, with the help of the motor pool sergeant, I carefully counted up all of the jeeps in our possession. I then ran quickly back to our captain and announced, "Sir, we currently have all of the jeeps that we are authorized to have. None are missing. So I don't know anything about a missing jeep." Problem resolved. It never came up again.

Soon after that my company traveled back to the coast and got a boat lift north to the sea port of Da Nang, followed by a short drive further north to Phu Bai. This was right at the peak of the Viet Cong's famous 1968 Tet offensive where they surrounded and overran the fortressed city of Hue just a few miles up the road from our base. It was a busy introduction to the war.

Thus began a yearlong combat assignment at the peak of the war effort in the busiest part of the combat zone where all of our troops were busy handling high priority message traffic 24/7. Each soldier in our company worked twelve hours at his duty assignment every day, seven days a week, without ever a break, and other assignments, like perimeter guard duty, on top of that. The pressure was relentless, but there was no alternative. This was war.

Prior to our arrival, the whole war effort was managed by General Westmoreland and his staff down in Saigon, but with the big build-up in Northern I Corps, they put together an Army Corps Headquarters there, led by General Abrams, second in command to Westmoreland, and so essentially our job was to provide all of the communications from General Abram's headquarters out to the various divisions and brigades in Northern I Corps. That included the 1st Air Cav Division, 101st Airborne Division, 82nd Airborne Division, 5th Mechanized Division, 1st Marine Division, 1st ARVN Division (Vietnamese), and brigades of the Americal Division among others. It was clearly a high stress environment. We were processing almost 1,000 messages per day – mostly Top Secret/High Priority classification - from our central communication center alone. Since all of my troops were working 12 hours a day at their duty stations, I told my non-commissioned officers that I expected 14 hours a day out of them, and 16 hours a day out of all of my officers. Of course, this meant really long days for me, too, seven days a week.

Interestingly, in my whole year in Vietnam, mostly spent working with other college-trained officers, I don't recall having had one single discussion dealing with the morality or political appropriateness of our country's involvement in Vietnam – a topic that was at the forefront of every political discussion back home at the time. I guess we all had only one single focus and that was to stay in one piece and get back home safely as soon as practical.

There was one highlight of my time in Vietnam and that was R & R. Once a year, when the command structure remembered, each GI was entitled to take a week off on R & R, Rest and Recuperation. And sometimes you even got to choose where to spend that R & R time. The choices included Bangkok, Thailand, Kuala Lumpur, Malaysia, Sydney, Australia, Honolulu, Hawaii, or Yokohama, Japan. When my turn came I chose Japan – with an eye toward using that time to climb 12,700 ft. high

Mt. Fuji. Going to Hawaii, was, of course, very popular since one could arrange to meet wives and family there, but I just couldn't bear seeing my wife Kay and eight month old Robin for a week, as much as I missed them both, and then have to leave again for another four or five months. So Japan it was. And I was fortunate enough to have arranged with an old friend, Bob Twist, from my time at Fort Huachuca, to join me on that R & R tour – with the intent of hiking up Mt. Fuji together.

It happened. Bob and I met up in Cam Ranh Bay, Vietnam, where he was stationed, flew to Yokohama, Japan, together, and, after a day spent buying all sorts of hi-fi equipment there and having it sent home, were soon off to Mt. Fuji. Of course, we had no idea how far away it was, how to actually get there, or how we were going to navigate our way up the mountain if we did manage to reach it.

I had figured out that the access road up the mountain started at a town called Kawaguchiko and so at the nearest train station I pointed out the town name on a map to the ticket agent and gave him a pile of Japanese yen. He didn't flinch, handed each of us three tickets, and carefully selected the required fee from our money pile – returning the rest.

Once inside the train station we approached the first local that we saw, showed her our tickets, and she graciously pointed us to the correct track for the start of our trip. It took nearly all day, but by late afternoon, and several train transfers later, we found ourselves at the town of Kawaguchiko, right at the base of Mt. Fuji. Bob opted for a hotel and dinner, but I was so psyched about climbing this mountain, and since we had already missed the last bus, I immediately started walking up the Mt. Fuji roadway. A nearby sign suggested that the end of the road was some twenty miles away – followed by an unknown number of miles more to the summit, but I didn't care. By golly I was on my way up Mt. Fuji. Very reluctantly, Bob decided that I needed adult supervision and so he followed me up the mountain complaining all the while.

In short order we came upon a building labeled Station #1. I immediately remembered having read somewhere that there were ten "stations" on the way to the summit. Heck, this must mean that we are already a tenth of the way to the top! I went into the station and saw that they had walking sticks for sale – complete with bells, ribbons, and a Japanese flag – and a brand. I soon came to understand that this "brand" was for having hiked up to and stopped at Station #1. Of course, I bought my own Mt. Fuji walking stick with visions of getting the other nine brands on my way up the mountain.

We were not actually very well equipped for climbing a serious, snow-covered volcano what with an Army field jacket, combat jungle boots, jeans, a gas mask bag for a day pack, an Army canteen for water, remnants of some C rations for food – and no flashlight. But onward and upward we went.

Around 8 or 9 PM we reached the end of the roadway, Station #5, after having hiked and hitchhiked over twenty miles, to find ourselves at a restaurant with lots of lights and excitement. We managed to order some tea and dinner by pointing at stuff that other diners were eating and wondered just what we were going to do now that it was dark and getting cold – and the restaurant was closing up for the night. Bob was getting less and less happy about our situation when, by luck, I befriended a young Japanese backpacker who I talked into heading up the mountain with us provided that we had use of his flashlight. As long as we kept moving we could stay warm I calculated, and so up we went.

Along the way we did see and inspect several more "stations," but none were manned and so we kept going. The well-worn trail was easy to see - just follow the garbage debris. It was actually somewhat shocking to see dozens and dozens of lunch packages dumped all over the otherwise pristine volcanic slopes of Mt. Fuji. Eventually, after many hours, we reached a "station" that was manned – by some workers who had been hired to repair sections of the hiking trail. And what a relief that was. They had a small charcoal fire going inside the hut to heat up water for tea, but it also heated up the hut as well, and so, for a change we were warm and comfortable. In fact, we even managed to nap a bit after having hiked all night long. And to my never ending delight, they managed to scour up a bunch of branding irons from under the hut's floor boards and commenced to fill my hiking pole with brands for all of the stations that we had passed – including a special brand that signified that I had reached the top – the crater rim itself. It turns out that, without knowing it, we had actually reached Station #10! We were only a short walk from the rim –

and the sun was just beginning to rise. What perfect timing. Of course, we immediately took off for the summit rim and witnessed a spectacular sunrise.

In that early morning light I could see the entire crater rim and could easily see that the rim's highest point was on the other side from where we were standing. I took off hiking, together with my Japanese friend, with a plan to quickly circle the entire rim, in order to reach the mountain's highpoint, while Bob declared that he was already on top of Mt. Fuji and no one could argue otherwise, and so he headed back to our warm hut with plans to meet me there later. So off I went – elated with our success.

In what seemed like a quick 45 minutes to an hour, I was back to my starting point, and equally quickly back inside our warm hut. But no Bob! His pack and expensive 35mm camera was still there, but not him. And the workers had not seen him.

I hung around for hours thinking that Bob had gone outside to relieve himself, got disoriented in the growing fog, and was having trouble finding his way back to the hut. While waiting for Bob to magically reappear, I entertained the laborers there by drawing a crude outline map in my notebook of the United States to try to show them where I lived. One of them immediately located New York, Chicago, and Los Angeles on my map, and one of the others, pointing to the area on my map where the Great Lakes were located, proceeded to name four of the five Great Lakes – looking at me then to see if I could name the fifth lake. Then he drew an outline of what I took to be Japan to see how good I was with Japanese geography. I quickly identified locations for Tokyo, Mt. Fuji, and Yokohama, but beyond that I was stumped. Of course I remembered the locations of Hiroshima and Nagasaki, the cities hit by our atomic bombs ending the war in the Pacific, but I thought it unwise to go there.

I stayed at the hut through most of that day before returning to Kawaguchiko for the night – returning back to the mountain all of the next day, but to no avail. There was no evidence of Bob anywhere. I took the train by myself back to Yokohama to report Bob as missing. He showed up unexpectedly at our base in Yokohama the following day, none the worse for wear, but having somehow lost his wallet along the way and having to bum money from total strangers for food and return train fare.

Sure enough, he had missed the hut high on the mountain because of the fog, got dis-oriented, and simply bailed off down the mountain hoping to somewhere intersect with our old trail, but ending up on the complete opposite side of the mountain from our ascent side. Such was our Mt. Fuji climbing experience.

Once back in Vietnam, the war continued to wear on with little to show for the anticipated peace agreement. In fact, after heated discussions that had gone on for many, many weeks in Paris by Henry Kissinger, our Secretary of State, and his North Vietnamese counterpart, they had finally agreed on the shape of the negotiating table. Now they were going to discuss the color of the table cloth for that table! I lost all hope of getting back home early.

Meanwhile our base at Phu Bai continued to come under regular enemy fire – mostly from 80 mm mortars and 4" rockets, and mostly at night. This seldom had any impact on our communications mission, since most all of our VHF radio equipment was in underground bunkers with only antennas and generators topside, but it did wreak havoc on our motor pool, mess hall, billets – and sleep.

Military activity throughout Northern I Corps remained very active throughout the balance of 1968, despite the peace talks being underway, which meant that our Signal Corps troops also remained very busy around the clock, seven days a week.

My remaining quarter of a year in Vietnam and in the Army continued to grind on with many incidents from the mundane to the bizarre. I got called out one night to deal with a young troop who had totally lost it and, for some unknown reason, borrowed one of our big trucks and plowed it into the unit's mess hall seriously damaging the mess hall and the truck. I interrogated this young soldier for the next 3 – 4 hours to try to get him to confess and to explain his behavior, but to no avail. Without an eye witness, we were not able to charge him with anything. And there was no mental health service to refer him to. The war continued on.

And on another night, when I was the assigned duty officer in charge, the sergeant of the guard reported that we had a young and very drunk Marine from an adjacent unit who was in our motor pool area shooting out all of our truck's lights and windshields! Of course, he expected me to deal with it since he wasn't excited about confronting a drunk marine with a loaded weapon. And since the motor pool was adjacent to our billeting area, there was always the chance that an errant bullet could strike one of our troops. I headed quickly over to the motor pool area, and after giving very explicit instructions to the sergeant of the guard as to what I expected of him, I confronted the Marine - instructing him in no uncertain terms, in my strongest officer voice, to immediately put down his rifle and step back. And, a bit to my surprise, he did! The sergeant immediately tackled him and we put him under arrest. I was very relieved! Then, out of the blue stepped a ranking Marine major who said that he would take care of the situation, took the guilty Marine from me – and put him to bed! I never heard anything further on the incident though I was much relieved to still be in one piece myself. The war continued on.

One afternoon, following an especially long period of 24 hour work days, I was walking up to the headquarters building, half in a daze, when I saw a dark green 1967 Ford station wagon, identical to the one that I owned back home. It was even the same year vintage. In my clouded mind I was sure that my wife Kay had driven over to Vietnam to pick me up. I walked immediately up to it and started opening the door to get in before waking up to reality and realized that that was only wishful thinking. A day later the car was gone – never to be seen again. None of my friends saw it and were sure that I only dreamed it. But I actually did see it. At least I'm pretty sure that I did. The war continued on.

On another night an enemy 80 mm mortar round, intended for the Corp headquarters building just down the street, fell short and landed instead on our mess hall – taking out our brand new, just delivered, ice cream-making machine. Talk about a morale hit! It wasn't repairable. Everyone was devastated. The war continued on.

A few weeks later I got orders to conduct a "line of duty" investigation involving an unfortunate friendly fire fatality that we suffered at one of our northern posts. This included a trip out to sea to one of our hospital ships to interview those who treated him and get a copy of the required paperwork. In the process, the ship's captain rounded me up to interview me as to the war's status back on the mainland. He and his hospital team saw the results of the war, treating all of the injured, but had very little view to what was actually happening on the ground. After briefing him, I got a personal invitation to have dinner with him and his staff since I was not able to arrange a flight back to the mainland until morning. What a spectacle that was! Here I found myself in the Officer's Mess, together with several ranking Navy officers, all in dress whites, joined by a dozen or so lovely Navy nurses, also in dress whites, at a table laid with fine white linens – and me in very dirty jungle fatigues in serious need of a shower. They all were, of course, completely cordial, and properly inquisitive, but I was totally ill at ease. When I left the table at the end of dinner, there were obvious dark smudges on the tablecloth where I had sat. In the morning I caught a flight back to the mainland. The war continued on.

On another occasion, at an evening staff meeting, our battalion commander interviewed all of us officers to see if anyone knew how a septic tank actually worked. (No, I don't make these things up!) It turned out that I was the only one who could explain to them all how it did. I got immediately charged with supervising a crew of young troops to dig a big hole in the ground and construct a septic tank, together with all of the concomitant plumbing – in order that the commander could have a flush toilet in his quarters! (The rest of us used a standard pit toilet.) I did supervise its build, but planned it so that it would very likely back up and stop working in about two months. (I was scheduled at that point to leave Vietnam in about two weeks.) The war continued on.

Late one night I was awakened to be told that I had lost one of my key communication stations in Dong Ha – which was a small coastal village further up north, within sight of the DMZ. An unlucky hit by an enemy 4 inch rocket had taken out my entire communications site even though it was well underground and covered by steel plates and four or five layers of sandbags. I was ordered to have replacements ready to fly in as soon as practical. I rounded up my sergeant and briefed him. He went to work immediately to gather up the required replacement transmitters, receivers, teletype and crypto gear, generators, and antennas, ammo, and rations and had them loaded on a truck, with a driver, to take them to our airstrip at first light. When I asked him about staffing, he had already compiled a list of those troops with the skills and experience that this assignment would require. But when I asked him who from that list he'd recommend for the assignment, he gave me a long look and quietly said, "Sir, they don't pay me enough to make those kinds of decisions." I made the selections from his list, with a heavy heart, and thanked him for his rapid response. He saluted me and left to notify the selected troops of their new assignment. I made the long walk to the airstrip to see them off, and the war continued on.

As I entered my final week in Vietnam, I became aware that one of our troops, in a field hospital in Cam Ranh Bay, had not gotten his monthly pay. So I graciously volunteered to fly down there and pay him. I packed very quickly, flew to Cam Ranh Bay on the first flight out, rounded him up in the hospital, had him paid in about 20 minutes, and then called my company commander to say that since I was "very close" to my scheduled departure flight anyway, I should just stay there until then. He agreed that that would be more efficient and so I ended up sitting on my thumbs for four days in the safety of that airbase and away from combat – and flew back home right on schedule – thankful to still be in one piece.

An interesting feature of that flight was that as I boarded the plane, a commercial Pan Am Airways Boeing 707, chartered by the military to shuttle troops to and from the US, the atmosphere was very somber; no one was talking. It was especially quiet; everyone seemed nervous. But upon take-off, just as the plane lifted off from the runway and flew over open water, there was an instantaneous and spontaneous cheering from everyone on board – all of the soldiers finally realizing that they had successfully survived their year in combat and were heading home. This jovial atmosphere continued for hours until we all fell asleep from long-term fatigue.

And then, many hours later, when the pilot came on the PA to announce that we could see the lights of Anchorage out of the window - the first sight of American soil in a year – there was, again, a spontaneous explosion of cheering from everyone – which generally continued until we reached our destination - the Seattle-Tacoma Airport. I was finally back in the US – still in one piece – and delighted for it. They tell me that the war continued on. It was November 1968.

Postscript: Upon arriving at Ft. Lewis, Washington, it was late in the evening, and so I was assigned a room in the post's officer's quarters for the night. I checked in and went straight to bed – still suffering fatigue. And, right at the crack of dawn, I was rudely awakened to the sound of two cannon blasts – right outside my room, and I immediately got out of my bed and dived under it – calling out "Incoming! Incoming!" as loud as I could – only a moment later to hear morning reveille being played over the post's PA system. I slowly realized that I was back in the US – and safe – and was only hearing the usual morning military flag raising ritual. (The post's flag pole and ceremonial cannons, I discovered, were right outside my window!)

Minutes later, as I entered the shower room down the hall, I heard a fellow tell his partner, "Must be another guy just back from Vietnam!" and he looked at me. I stared right back and just said, "Yea, I heard that, too. Glad it wasn't me."

Alaskan Mountain Goat Hunt

A long time Arizona friend, Gene Davison, introduced me to hunting back in 1978. I quickly embraced it because it provided yet another good excuse to spend time outdoors. My introduction started with the state's annual fall dove and quail hunting seasons, but quickly spread to deer and javelina hunting as well. I even had success with hunting desert pronghorn (antelope).

A couple times I even tried my hand at bear hunting. That means that you buy a bear tag and go out into the woods during bear season – and wear out a lot of shoe leather getting lost in the woods in areas where no self-respecting bear would ever be caught in.

Elk hunting was another matter. I tagged along on a successful elk hunt or two in southern Colorado with Gene and quickly discovered that a full-grown bull elk comes in an awfully big package! I could just imagine stumbling around in the dark timber one day and running into one. It would likely have a heart attack in front of me, fall over dead, and I'd be stuck with so much meat that I'd need a four-wheel drive forklift to retrieve it. And I didn't want to even think about how many years it would take to actually eat that much meat.

But then, around a campfire late one night, Gene proposed that we go on a "real" hunt up into the wilds of Alaska – "where men are men!"

Since Gene had lived and worked up there in an earlier life, I told him to set it up and I'd go with him. I'm not sure that I expected this to ever happen, but Gene made contact with Larry Ethelbah, an old Arizona friend who was working for the U.S. Forest Service out of Petersburg, Alaska. Larry quickly invited us up to his place and offered to help set it all up. The popular species to hunt in Alaska were caribou, bighorn sheep and grizzly, but since they were prohibitively expensive for a non-resident license and tag, and we wanted to do this hunt on the cheap, we opted for mountain goat. Larry liked this idea, too, because he knew of several areas that were rich in mountain goats within an hour's flight into the back country east of Petersburg. He even managed to loan us several recent Forest Service aerial photos of the area to help keep us oriented.

In August 1984 Gene and I flew from Tucson, Arizona, to Petersburg, Alaska, on the daily "milk run" flight out of Seattle with stops along the way in Wrangell and Ketchikan. Petersburg was a bit of a surprise. Originally settled by Russians, it had been rebuilt long ago by fishermen from Scandinavia and still showed signs of classic Scandinavian house construction and decoration. Another surprise was that every family had at least one or two cars and the streets were very busy even though there is only one road – and it's less than two miles long - and a second road to the airport that was only ¼ mile away! There are no roads in or out of the city to anywhere else in the world.

Day 1: Our original plan had been to spend the first day or two visiting, getting our hunting licenses and permits, re-packing, and studying a variety of maps of the area. But Larry found us a pilot who would fly us into the interior for only $90/hour – half the normal fee – provided that we could leave that very afternoon. Being cheap, we rushed to get our non-resident hunting licenses ($60/each) and mountain goat tag ($250/each), re-packed, bought some last minute food, and were soon on our way to Goat Lake in the interior, east of Petersburg, just above the Stikine River.

At Goat Lake our pilot dropped us off on a six foot-by-six foot shore, wished us luck, promised to return someday, and flew out. We barely had enough room to put on mosquito repellant and head nets, and then prepare our packs, rifles, and boots for what was going to be a very steep, wet, rough, over-grown, rocky slope up to goat country. I, of course, got volunteered to be the one to climb one of the tall trees on our tiny spot of land in order to stash our spare food, fuel, and ammunition.

Our uphill route turned out to be torturously steep, heavily overgrown, wet, and very slippery. And we needed to get up at least 1,000 ft. to have any hope of having a horizontal place on which to set up our tents – all the while continuously looking out for bears.

We started up this difficult slope at 5 PM with heavy packs loaded with our hunting and camping gear and 5 - 6 days' worth of food. It wasn't until after 10 PM that I found a "level" spot that would hold my tent for the night. It was right at snow line – with large fields of steep snow above me. I was alone and soaking wet with temperatures in the mid-40's F. The mosquitoes were so thick that they formed a cloud around me – and moved right with me as I moved about. I prepared and ate my dinner in the dark.

Day 2: It turned out to have been a terrible spot for a tent, and so I promised myself that the first order of business in the morning would be to re-site it to a better location. In fact, though, two weeks later, the tent was still in its original location. I never did manage to find a better spot for it. This might be excellent mountain goat country, but it sure was not excellent camping country. It had been raining off and on all day long. And we had chosen this time of the year because this was Alaska's "dry season!" Gene showed up mid-morning – having spent the night in a spot even worse than mine. He also was soaking wet. We were clearly off to a great start!

After some lunch we headed up into the adjacent snow fields, complete with crampons on our boots, split up, and began hunting. Within that first hour I spotted a tiny white spot on a steep slope of green grass a long ways out. With binoculars I confirmed that, in fact, it was a mountain goat, but I could not see if it was a billy (male) or nanny (female) (and my permit was only good for hunting full grown billies). I laid out a long route to the high ridge that looked down on that patch of grass and headed out hoping to not startle the goat before I could get close enough for a shot – if it turned out to be a billy.

I had read in Douglas Chadwick's book on mountain goats, "A Beast the Color of Winter," that they spend 70 percent of their life on slopes whose overall angle was steeper than 40 degrees, that is, above the angle of repose, and the remainder of their time on meadows and talus near these slopes. Their only serious predators should be bears and mountain lions – which should always come from below them. So my intent was to get above this goat and hope that he had read the same book and wouldn't be concerned about noises and movement from above him.

By the time that I reached the vicinity of this goat, an hour later, still well above him, I confirmed that it was a mature billy and so I began cautiously moving down slope toward him hoping to get within shooting range before scaring him off. Of course, "moving cautiously" here was much like tiptoeing down a huge pile of marbles – all loose, noisy, and treacherous. But somehow I did get within about 250 yards of him, took my shot, and downed him.

I was, of course, elated with my hunting success because I had gotten what I came here to get. I thought that even Larry Ethelbah would be impressed with this quick success. But it also occurred to me that I now had almost two weeks to sit on my thumbs with very little to do beyond swatting mosquitoes.

I quickly field dressed the goat and took off for camp in the setting sun – reaching it by about 9 PM. Gene had also seen goats that day – maybe eight or nine of them. So, Larry was right; this was a good place to hunt goats. The weather had looked ominous all day long, but it never did rain on us. We had a quick dinner and turned in just before 11 PM – totally worn out.

Day 3: I was up by 6 AM to clear skies and was on my way back up to my goat before 8 AM – reaching it just before 11 AM – again soaking wet from sweat. A stiff breeze temporarily drove off the mosquitoes and I could, for the first time, look around without my head net on. That was a brief but welcome relief.

I had my goat skinned, quartered, and hidden in a small glacier snow cave nearby and was headed back to camp by 3:30 PM in sunshine and mostly blue skies. My plan was to bring my pack next time and start hauling out the meat. I met up with Gene and he and I arrived back at camp around 8 PM – with foul weather moving in. After a study of my goat's head and horns, which I had brought back with me, we decided that my mountain goat was a mature six year old billy. That's when I discovered that my water bottle had sprung a leak. My pack was now a Kool Aid strawberry pink! I had a second water bottle, but, of course, it was back down at our stash at Goat Lake. I turned in at 10 PM – still elated with my hunting success.

Day 4: Sat in the tent all day long while it rained. I spent the day sleeping, reading, and swatting mosquitoes. It was impossible to leave the tent for any reason and return without bringing back in a couple hundred mosquitoes with me. That was getting to be a real nuisance! I did have some "mosquito coils" with me that, when lit, emitted a smoke that killed the mosquitoes, so that helped me manage the mosquito population inside the tent. But I had to go through this ritual every time that I returned to the tent after having been outside for any reason. The rain held off just long enough to have dinner and then started up again.

Day 5: We were starting to get low on food, and so I made a trip back down that dreaded trail to Goat Lake for more supplies for the two of us from our tree stash. I was happy to confirm that it was still intact. Meanwhile Gene moved his entire camp up onto the high ridge. He wanted to avoid having to climb up onto the ridge every morning since that took him several hours every day. From now on I would be by myself at my camp. That was not something that I was looking forward to. I was back from my trip to Goat Lake by 11 AM in time for lunch and then hiked, in the rain, back to my glacier where I had stored the goat meat in order to begin hauling it out – only to discover that a bear had found my meat and run off with all four quarters. The entire glacier surface was covered with fresh bear tracks going every which way. I eventually managed to find the two hind quarters where they had gotten dropped into a large hole in the snowfield, but never did locate the two front quarters.

Recovering these two rear quarters from down in the hole turned out to be no small challenge since I didn't have any climbing rope with me. But I did eventually retrieve them. (It briefly occurred to me that if I was not able to get back out of this hole, it might very well be days before Gene even missed me – let alone start looking for me.) I quickly boned out those two quarters, with one eye over my shoulder looking for bears since I had left my rifle in my tent to lighten my load. At this point I was starting to really miss it since now I knew that there was a bear in the neighborhood!

On my way back to my camp I saw Gene take a couple shots at some goats, but missed them. We searched and searched for them, but they had vanished. I returned to my camp – in the rain – and stashed my meat in a nearby snowfield. The rain had continued all afternoon and evening. It was not fun at all. I figured out how to cook my dinner and eat it totally inside my small tent. This was very risky, but it was sure nice, for a change, to prepare and eat dinner without mosquitoes to swat. It was a lonely camp though.

Day 6: It rained all day long; and all night, too, with temperatures in the low to mid-40's. Nothing to do but sit it out. I was serenaded that evening by marmots whistling all around me. I wonder how they deal with the merciless mosquitoes?

Day 7: Still raining. Made a trip up to Gene's camp to council. On our original plan we had worried that we just might not see any goats at all - in which case we didn't want to spend our entire two weeks at only one camp, and so we had asked our pilot to fly back in on our Day 8 in order to have an option of flying us somewhere else for the balance of our trip. But Gene was still seeing goats here so he had no reason to go anyplace else. That meant that I would have to once more trudge back down to Goat Lake to meet our pilot, ask him to fly out my goat meat so that it could get refrigerated back in Petersburg, and schedule his return flight in another four days. It would sure be tempting to just get on that plane and return to the land of hot showers, warm and comfortable beds, dry clothes, and no mosquitoes!

Day 8: Woke up to cloudy, foggy, rainy weather for my trek back down to Goat Lake – loaded with mountain goat meat. The plane arrived at 1 PM and we agreed on a new plan. After the plane left I went through all of our remaining food supplies in our tree stash and carried all of it back up to my camp – arriving there by 3:00 PM. That climb sure wasn't getting any easier. And I was, once more, soaking wet. Clouds were very heavy, but they delivered only a little rain that day. I estimated that Gene and I both had enough food to get us halfway through Day 11 – with the plane scheduled to return on Day 12.

Day 9: After dragging my feet for a few hours waiting for the heavy fog to lift, I trudged up to Gene's camp with all of his remaining food. I stayed up there for several hours looking for goats for Gene to hunt, but never saw any. As a reward for bringing Gene all of his remaining food from our Goat Lake reserve, he gave me two candles, a package of M & M's, and some brandy. That almost made it worth the trip down to the lake and back. I even managed to get my shirt and pants dried out finally. I was set. I returned to my camp by 7 PM and shortly after that heard Gene take a number of shots.

Day 10: Awoke to sunshine, but it quickly changed back to rain during breakfast. I forced myself to climb once more up the ridge to see if Gene needed a hand with anything. Turns out that he was pretty sure that he had hit one of the mountain goats that he shot at last evening, but, if he did, it managed to get away from him. We hiked around all day long in the fog and rain, but never caught any sight of it. I was back to my camp by 6 PM soaking wet. I was beginning to wonder what it felt like to actually be dry all day long.

Day 11: Rained all night long and then, in the morning, decreased to a continuous drizzle with the upper ridge totally fogged in. Just where is all of this rain coming from? Clearing skies around 2 PM allowed me to start getting some of my clothing dried out. And then it started drizzling again. This near continuous rain was starting to get really old! And I had finished reading the last of my books, as well as all of Gene's books, and there was little else to do. This mountain goat terrain is certainly more difficult to get around in than typical big horn sheep country, and so I was not able to do much exploring. From some vantage points I was able to see the Stikine River far below us, but I was never sure if I could actually hike to it if it were necessary because it was so steep and overgrown. Even in good weather it would have been difficult to get more than a handful of miles from camp without dropping into the nearly impenetrable "jungle" that surrounded these peaks.

Day 12: Up at 6:00 AM to blue skies and sunshine – for a change. Had breakfast and was fully packed in a flash. We started back down to Goat Lake as soon as Gene arrived from his high aerie up on the ridge. Our remaining food reserves were down to one package of instant oatmeal, some M&M's, and two tea bags. We couldn't have stayed much longer. Our plane arrived in mid-afternoon and we were soon back in Petersburg – much relieved. That was about all of the fun that I could stand and quickly decided that I wouldn't be in a rush to repeat the experience.

Chapter Eight

In Closing

Well, at some point I need to wrap this up. What did I fail to mention? It can't be much. How about the almost three dozen week long bike tours that I participated in around the western states. They were all pretty routine – except for the one in Oregon where we actually lost a cyclist. No, I don't mean that he went the wrong way and got lost. He actually disappeared! One day mid-week he had finished his ride for the day, secured his bike, set up his tent, showered and changed, and then simply disappeared – leaving behind his duffel, bike, tent, clothes, wallet, money and even charge cards – and was never seen from again.

Or the time in Colorado, on the commercial Bicycle Tour of Colorado, in July, when a freak snowstorm between Ouray and Durango caused the state police to shut down the entire roadway forcing everyone to "hole up" in Silverton until buses could be secured to shuttle us safely to our destination – except that a very few of us, including me, somehow missed getting the word, and rode on to Durango nearly freezing to death on icy roads.

Or the time on our bike tour across northern Nevada on Highway US 50, the country's "loneliest highway" where each day we were alerted to one "exciting feature" of the day. One day our "exciting feature" was the famous Nevada "shoe tree" – the only tree in all 50 states to make it onto that state's official road map. What did it look like? Well, picture a large tree with lots of shoes hanging in it! Exciting? Or how about riding by the official Top Gun Bombing Range? What did it look like? Well, when they are not bombing, it looked pretty much like all of the rest of Nevada! Or how about visiting three or four of the old 19th Century Pony Express stations? Of course, the only thing left any longer is a couple bushels of rocks left in a pile off the side of the road at each spot. Or the brand new nine bay fire station, filled with brand new fire trucks, to handle possible fires in a village of population 150. (Could we figure out what the town did with their property tax receipts when the town's tax base included a very large and successful mining operation?) Or a gas station/bar/motel/gift shop/gambling casino right on the Nevada-Utah border – with the casino on the Nevada side where gambling is legal and the gas pumps on the Utah side where the state gas tax was lower.

Or the time on our bike tour in California when our campsite was overrun with peacocks. Strikingly beautiful as they were in the day time, their strident calls throughout the middle of the night kept us awake all night long.

Or the time I cycled down the length of New Zealand's north and south islands in 1999, or cycled in northern Italy during their famous 2007 Giro d'Italia bike race, or bike toured the Dalmatian Islands of Croatia and through the many historic Inca ruins of Peru in 2016 or across Botswana, Namibia, and South Africa in 2017.

Or the time I cycled across the US from the Pacific on the shores of Oregon to the Atlantic on the shores of New Hampshire in 2009.

Or the time that I skied, with backpack, along with a bunch of friends, to the North Rim of the Grand Canyon in the middle of winter and continued on down to the Phantom Ranch at the Colorado River, and up to the South Rim – and had so much fun doing it that we repeated it two more times in subsequent years.

Or the time that I made an attempt to climb Cho Oyo, an 8,000 meter peak in the Tibetan Himalaya, in 2006. Or, over any number of years, I managed to climb forty four of Colorado's fifty eight 14,000 ft. Rocky Mountain peaks. Or numerous backpack trips with son Scott down Arizona's Paria Canyon or into Colorado's Weminuche Wilderness.

Or the time on our bike tour in New Mexico when we were riding around the Enchanted Circle, on the advice of a friend, I stopped to visit a memorial chapel and visitor center that had been built by a local doctor to honor his son who had lost his life in Vietnam – very close to the time and place where I had been stationed when I was there. It was the most emotionally moving post-Vietnam experience of my life. After several failed attempts to enter either facility, I was finally successful only when a friend came by who could escort me. Once inside the visitor center I encountered an elderly gentleman who, after one look at me, simply said, "When were you there?" He was the boy's father. It was very moving.

But I don't have time or space for all of those stories, so they will have to await another venue. Living out my own personal mid-life crisis with breathtaking domestic and international outdoor adventures was a journey I wouldn't have missed for anything. Not for everyone, I suppose, but it worked for me.

Appendix

Mountain Climbing

2015:

Climbed six 14,000 ft peaks in Colorado

2014:

Mt. Vinson   16,160 ft   Antarctica

2013:

Hiked Arizona's Grand Canyon Rim-to-Rim-to-Rim Route

Climbed four 14,000 ft peaks in Colorado

2012:

Tocllaraju (19,785 ft) Ishinca (18,138 ft) Peru

Climbed seven 14,000 ft peaks in Colorado

2011:

Climbed seven 14,000 ft peaks in Colorado and California

2008:

Huayna Potosi (19,890 ft)   Pequeno Alpamayo (17,721 ft)   Bolivia

Cerro Ventanani (17,846 ft) Pico Mirador (17325 ft)   "

Chacaltaya (17,803 ft)   "

2007:

Chimborazo (20,703 ft)	Cotopaxi (19343 ft)	Ecuador
Iliniza Sur (17,267 ft)	Corazon (15,800 ft)	"
Rucu Pichincha (15,413 ft)	Pasochoa (13,776 ft)	"

2006:

Cho Oyu	to 22,000 ft	Tibet
Kings Peak	13,528 ft	Utah

2005:

Redcloud, Sunshine Peaks	14,000+ ft	Colorado
Mt. Rainier	14,410 ft	Washington
Borah Peak	12,662 ft	Idaho
Grosglockner (12,461 ft)	Kleinglockner (12,411 ft)	Austria

Cayambe(18,993 ft)	Iliniza Norte(16,794 ft)	Ecuador
Guagua Pichincha(15,728 ft)		"

2004:

Rifflehorn(9,600 ft)	Wellenkuppe(12,802 ft)	Switzerland
Zinalrothorn(13,845 ft)	Breithorn (traverse) (13,658 ft)	"
Allalinhorn (traverse) (13,209 ft		"

2003:

Two weeks in Patagonia, Argentina attempting Cerro Marconi Norte & Punta Fina

Climbed sixteen 14,000 ft peaks in Colorado

Mt. Kilimanjaro	19,340 ft (second ascent)	Tanzania

2002:

Jungfrau(13,642 ft)	Dufourspitze (Monte Rosa) (15,204 ft)	Switzerland
Mont Blanc	15,771 ft	France

2000:

Windom, Sunlight, Eolus Peaks   14,000+ ft   Colorado

1999:

Mt. Shasta, Mt. Sill, Split Mountain	14,000+ ft	California
Mt. Hood	11,239 ft	Oregon
Boundary Peak	13,140 ft	Nevada
Gannett Peak	13,804 ft	Wyoming
Granite Peak	12,799 ft	Montana

1993:

Carstensz Pyramid	16,023 ft	Papua, Indonesia

1992:

Grand Teton	13,770 ft	Wyoming
Ama Dablam	to 20,000 ft	Nepal

Climb aborted due to climber accident / rescue

Kala Patthar	18,514 ft	Nepal

1991:

Mt. Elbrus   18,481 ft   Russia

1990:

Mt. Kilimanjaro   19,340 ft   Tanzania

Aconcagua   22,830 ft   Argentina

1989:

Pico de Orizaba (18,700 ft)   Popocatepetl (17,900 ft)   Mexico

Ixtaccihuatl (17,300 ft)   "

1987:

McKinley (Denali)   20,310 ft   Alaska

1979 – 1986:

Nineteen climbs of thirteen 14,000 ft peaks in Colorado and California

1968:

Mt.Fuji   12,700 ft   Japan

www.ingramcontent.com/pod-product-compliance
Lightning Source LLC
Chambersburg PA
CBHW041627140626
46547CB00031B/1129